CAMPFIRE RECIPES

50 + Comfort and Satisfying Camping Recipes

(The Family Camping Guide & the Camping Cookbook)

Kenya Epling

Published by Alex Howard

© **Kenya Epling**

All Rights Reserved

Campfire Recipes: 50 + Comfort and Satisfying Camping Recipes (The Family Camping Guide & the Camping Cookbook)

ISBN 978-1-990169-45-8

All rights reserved. No part of this guide may be reproduced in any form without permission in writing from the publisher except in the case of brief quotations embodied in critical articles or reviews.

Legal & Disclaimer

The information contained in this book is not designed to replace or take the place of any form of medicine or professional medical advice. The information in this book has been provided for educational and entertainment purposes only.

The information contained in this book has been compiled from sources deemed reliable, and it is accurate to the best of the Author's knowledge; however, the Author cannot guarantee its accuracy and validity and cannot be held liable for any errors or omissions. Changes are periodically made to this book. You must consult your doctor or get professional medical advice before using any of the suggested remedies, techniques, or information in this book.

Table of contents

PART 1 1

INTRODUCTION 2

CHAPTER 1: BREAKFAST CAMPING RECIPES 3

CHEESE, BACON AND HAM IN BOAT POTATO 3
BREAKFAST ÉCLAIRS 3
APPLE CRISP OVER COALS 5
STEWED BEANS AND SAUSAGE 6
PRESSED ITALIAN SANDWICHES 7
BREAKFAST BURRITOS 8
LUMBERJACK BREAKFAST FOIL PACK 9
BREAKFAST POTATO FRITTATA 10
PROTEIN RICH BREAKFAST MUFFIN 11
CHAPTER 2: MAIN MEAL CAMPING RECIPES 12
QUESADILLAS 12
FOIL WRAPPED HERBY SALMON 12
NACHOS PIZZA STYLE 14
BALSAMIC GRILLED VEGETABLES 15
WHOLE WHEAT PASTA IN FOIL 16
BARBECUED SALMON 17
RICE AND CHICKEN PAELLA STYLE 18
CAMP PIZZA 20
PEPPER AND LIMED GRILLED CHICKEN BREASTS 21
SMOKED CHILI, BACON AND BEEF STEW 22
MUSHROOM CAMPFIRE FOIL PACKET 23
CAMPFIRE CHICKEN STEW 23
BALSAMIC STEAK 24
CAJUN SHRIMP GUMBO 25
BLUE CHEESE BURGER STEAKS 26

CHAPTER 3: CAMPFIRE SNACK RECIPES 27

GRILLED BLUEBERRY COBBLER 27
CHOCO-MALLOWS IN BANANA SLIT 27

Fruit & S'more Cones 28
Blueberry Muffin in Orange Balls 28
Orange-y Cinnamon Rolls 29
Hot Dog on Sticks with Bread 29
Pound Cake S'mores 31
Oreo S'mores 32

CAMPING RECIPES 67

Bacon, Egg, Sausage and Potato Omelet 67
Balsamic Barbecued Steak 67
BBQ Beef Ribs 69
BBQ Chicken 69
Beans and Franks 71
Breakfast Burritos 71
Campfire Baked Potato 73
Clam Chowder 73
Dutch Oven Baked Beans 75
Dutch Oven Cinnamon Caramel Monkey Bread 75
Dutch Oven Chili Macaroni 77
Dutch Oven Fruit Pie 77
Eggs in a Nest 79
Fire-Roasted Cinnamon Apple 79
Five Alarm Dutch Oven Chili 81
Killer Kabobs 82
Quick and Easy Pancakes 82
Traditional Banana Boat 83

BONUS CHAPTER: CAMPFIRE DESSERTS 85

Banana Boats 85
Chocolate Banana Burritos 87
Cinnamon-Sugar Apple Sauce 87
Coconut Bread 89
Ice Chest Fudge 89
Orange Brownies 90
Orange Cupcakes 91
Oreo Pudding Pie 91

Personal Fruit Pies	93
Pineapple Donut Delight	93
Rocky Road Cones	94
S'Mores	94
Strawberry S'Mores	95

PART 2 96

MAIN DISHES 97

30 Minute Goulash	97
A Mean Three-Bean Salad	98
Ain't Plain Mashed Potatoes	98
All Fruit Salad	99
All in One Burger and Sides	100
Amarillo Steak	100
Antipasta Dip	101
Arkansas Potatoes	101
Asian Marinade	102
Aunt Karnie's Pasta Salad	102
"Auntie Jillaine's" Newyork/Maryland Crab Cakes	103
Awesome Chip or Vegetable Dip	103
Baby Red Potatoes	104
Backwoods Chili Rice Skillet	104
Bacon & Cheddar Grilled Cheese Sandwich	105
Bacon Tortilla Rolls	105
Baked Beans	106
Baked Lima Beans	106
Baked Onions	106
Baked Potato in a Can	107
Baked Santa Fe Dip	107
Balsamic Steak	108
Balsamic Vinegar Chicken	109
Bar B Que Mushrooms	109
Barbecue Sandwiches	110
Barbecued Chipped Ham Sandwich	110
Barbecued Chopped Ham Sandwich	111
Bar-B-Que Bean Bake	111

BBQ Bacon-Wrapped Stuffed Shrimp 112
BBQ Baked Beans 112
BBQ Beef Sandwiches 113
BBQ Country Style Ribs 113
BBQ Pitas 114
BBQ Potato Chips 115
BBQ Ribs 115
Bean & Cornbread Casserole 116
Beef in the Wild 117
Beefy 5 Can Soup 117
Big Jim's Camping Beans 118
Black Bean Soup 118
Blair's Campfire Stew 119
Bob's Simple Skillet Supper 119
Bourbon Steak (Or Chicken) Marinade 120
Bratwurts & Swiss 121
Broccoli Cole Slaw 121
Broccoli-Chicken Casserole 121
Brownie's Chili, Cheese & Rice 122
Brunswick Stew 122
Bunless Hot Dogs 123
Burger & Veggie Pouches 124
Burn-side taters 124
Cabbage Lasagna 125
Cabbage Salad 125
Cajun Shrimp Gumbo 126
California Egg Crunch 127
Camp Beef Brisket 127
Camp Bread 128
Camp Fire Rainbow Trout 129
Camp Stew 129
Camp Stove Goulash 129
Camo Tacos 130
Camp Taters 131
Camper Casserole 131
Camper Goulash 131

Camper's Beans	132
Camper's Luau Chicken	132
Camper's Pizza Skillet Delight	133
Campers Stew	134
Campfire Chicken and Vegetables	134
Campfire Chicken and Veggies	135
Campfire Chicken Pot Pie	135
Campfire Chicken	136
Campfire Chili with Hamburger	137
Campfire Chili	137
Campfire Corn on the Cob	138
Campfire Corn	138
Campfire Dinner	139
Campfire French Fries	139
Campfire Onion	140
Campfire Pizza's	140
Campfire Potatoes and Onions	141
Campfire Potatoes	141
Campfire Roasted Turkey	142
Campfire Squash	142
Campfire Stew with Hamburger	143
Campfire Stew	143
Campfire Stir Fry	143
Campfire Sweet Potatoes	144
Campfire Tacos	145
Campfire Vegetable Packet	145
Campfire Zucchini	146
Campground Chicken Salad	146
Campgruond Goodies	147
Campground Stew	147
Camping Burritos	147
Camping Potatoes	148
Camping Spaghetti	149
Camping Stew	149
Camp-Out Chicken	150
Camp-Out Tomatoes	150

Can-Do Potato Bean Salad	151
Carrot and Egg Salad	151
Cashew Apple Salad	152
Cheddar spam and potatoes	152
Cheddar Tator Tot Casserole	152
Cheese on the Cob	153
Cheesy Sausage Skillet	153
Cheesy Veggie Chowder	154
Cherry Fruit Salad	154
Chicken & Rice	155
Chicken Almondine	155
Chicken & Corn Soup	156
Chicken and Stuffing	156
Chicken Asparagus	157
Chicken Broccoli Casserole	157
Chicken Cacciatore	159
Chicken in A Bag	159
Chicken kabob wraps on flat bread	160
Chicken Mole	161
Chicken or Pork Chops Deluxe	162
Chicken Pie	162
Chicken Pockets	162
Chicken Pot Pie	163
Chicken Salad for Two	163
Chicken Salad	164
Chicken Salsa Stir-fry	164
Chicken Sandwiches	165
Chicken Sausage Bake	165
Chicken Vegetable Medley	166
Chicken Wing Dip	166
Chicken with Wine and Capers	167
Chicken/Veggie Pouches	168
Chili Bean Bake	168
Chili Bean Soup	169
Chili cheese dog casserole	170
Chili Cheeseburger	170

Chili Dog Casserole	171
Chili Dogs in a Blanket	171
Chinese Cabbage Slaw	172
Chinese chicken salad with chicken strips	173
Chinese Chicken Salad	174
Chinese Vermicelli	174
Chuck Wagon Dinner	175
Chuck Wagon	175
Chunky Chili Chaser	176
Citrus Rainbow Trout	176
Civiche	177
Clam Chowder	177
Corn Bread Salad	178
Corn Cassarole	178
Corn Casserole	179
Corn Chips	179
Corn on the Cob with Bacon	180
Corn on the Cob	180
Corn Roasted In Foil on Coals	181
Corn Roasted On Grill over Coals	181
Corn Souffle	182
Crab Meat Appetizer	182
Crunchy Oriental Coleslaw Salad	183
Cucumber Salad	183
Curry Chicken Salad	184
Dave's Sweet BBQ Corn on the Cob	185
Deluxe Steamed Green Beans	185
Dilled Peas & Potatoes	186
Doctored Up Pork & Beans	186
Dutch oven Stuffed Peppers	187
Easy Barbecue Sauce	187

Part 1

Introduction

When it comes to camping a lot of us make do without the comforts of living in a house and commonly we resign ourselves to overcooked meals or undercooked meals, and canned meals. However, this should not be the case. If you are a savvy eater, then don't let camping get in between your desire for good food and getting it.

This book will help you plan camping meals and even teach you how to make chef worthy meals while camping. So, let's not waste precious words with trying to entice you with how good camping meals can get with these secret recipes that I will share with you. Instead, let's get right on to the recipes!

Chapter 1: Breakfast Camping Recipes

Cheese, Bacon and Ham in Boat Potato

To make this an easy camping recipe, I suggest that you bake the potatoes while still at home. Potatoes should be big and long, around 5 inches. This recipe is good for 2 persons.
Ingredients:
1 large baked potato with skin, 5 inches long
4 ham slices
4 bacon slices
1 stalk green onion, sliced
2 tbsps sour cream
4 cheese slices of choices, provolone is suggested
Directions:

1)Sliced the baked potato, into 4 equal slices.
2)Place 1 ham slice, 1 cheese slice and 1 bacon slice inside each potato slice. Repeat process for remaining slices.
3) Wrap boat potato in foil greased with cooking spray and grill on a campfire for 20 minutes until bacon is cooked and cheese is melted.

Breakfast Éclairs

To make this éclair perfectly, use a clean stick at least 1-inch in diameter, a wooden dowel would do the trick perfectly. One recipe can create at least 6-8 éclairs. If reusing a dowel, grease before each use.
Ingredients:
Spray whip cream
Nutella or chocolate frosting
Vanilla snack pack pudding, or any flavor

Refrigerated crescent rolls

Directions:

1)Grease the top of a wooden dowel with oil until 3-4 inches of its length.
2)Slice off 1 serving of crescent roll and wrap around a greased wooden dowel. Cover the tip of the dowel with dough and at least 2-inches or more of the length of the dowel.
3) Repeat the process with other crescent roll serving and dowels.
4)Cook over campfire until dough is golden brown. Remove the cooked dough by sliding it off the dowel. Be careful as the dough is hot.
5)Inside the hole of the éclair (created by the dowel), add your choice of pudding. Slather Nutella or chocolate frosting on top of the éclair and if desired top with whip cream. Enjoy!

Apple Crisp over Coals

This recipe can be prepared ahead of time or while still in your home. So that once in the campsite, all you have to do is pop this in the BBQ pit.

Ingredients:
Squeeze of a lemon juice
3 Apples
2 tbsps butter, plus more for foil
Dash of nutmeg
¼ tsp cinnamon
¼ cup granulated sugar
3 tbsps packed brown sugar
6 tbsps flour
½ cup old-fashioned oats

Directions:

1) Cut 2 pieces of 15-inch (or more) long foil.
2) Place 1 foil on a table and grease with butter. Add nutmeg, cinnamon, sugars, flour and oats. Toss to mix.
3) Add butter to mixture and mix with hands to make a crumbly batter.
4) Core and slice the apples in to thin slices. Add squeeze of lemon and mix.
5) In the other piece of foil, grease with butter. Add the apples in the middle. Pour in the crumbly oat mixture and cover with the foil. Seal the edges of the foil well.
6) Barbecue for 20 minutes, with apple slices on bottom and near fire. Best served with a scoop of ice cream if available.

Stewed Beans and Sausage

For this recipe to be perfectly made, a cast iron camp Dutch oven is needed.

Ingredients:
¼ cup fresh oregano leaves
1 ½ lbs Aidell's Italian sausage, sliced into 1-inch thick
4 medium garlic cloves, chopped
1 poblano chile, sliced
½ yellow bell pepper, sliced
½ red bell pepper, sliced
1 tbsp chopped fresh rosemary leaves
1/3 cup olive oil
1 can (15.5-oz) cannellini beans, drained and rinsed
1 15.5-oz can chickpeas, drained and rinsed

Directions:
1) In Dutch oven, place all ingredients except for oregano. Add ¾ cup water, cover and place in low campfire.
2) Occasionally stir stew every 10 minutes. If water runs out, just add ½ cup of water each time.
3) Stew is cooked after 30-45 minutes of cooking time or once sausages are swollen and peppers are soft.
4) Once cooked, remove from fire and stir in oregano, serve and enjoy.

Pressed Italian Sandwiches

For a perfect pressed sandwich, a campfire cast iron Panini maker is your best friend. But, innovativeness is also key to this dish if you don't have a sandwich maker on hand.

Ingredients:
Freshly ground black pepper
6 leaves fresh basil, torn into bite sized pieces
1 roasted red bell pepper, chopped
8-oz fresh mozzarella, sliced
¼ lb thinly sliced spicy Italian cold cuts
3-oz thinly sliced prosciutto
¼ lb thinly sliced Genoa salami
2 tbsps extra virgin olive oil
2 tbsps balsamic vinegar
½ cup store-bought black or green olive tapenade
1 ciabatta load, cut lengthwise

Directions:
1) Drizzle with oil and vinegar the top side half of loaf. On bottom half, spread with tapenade.
2) On top of tapenade, layer basil, red pepper, cold cuts, mozzarella, salami and prosciutto.
3) Sprinkle with pepper and cover with top half of loaf. Cut in half and place inside a cast iron panini maker and grill over campfire for 3 minutes per side or more, until ciabatta is crisped and lightly browned and cheese is melted. If you don't have a Panini griller you can use a cast iron skillet and lightly grease with oil. Preheat skillet before adding your ciabatta. Cook for 3 minutes per side while pressing down on the sandwich with a cooking spoon or fork.

Breakfast Burritos

To make this burrito easier to make, I suggest boil your potatoes at home and season with pepper and salt. Place in a zip lock bag. Also cook in advance breakfast sausage, crumble and add into bag of potatoes. Recipe below is good for 1 burrito.

Ingredients:
Salsa or hot sauce, optional
¼ cup grated cheddar cheese
¼ cup crumbled and browned breakfast sausage
1 tbsp green onions
2 eggs lightly beaten
Pepper and salt to taste
1 Yukon gold potato, peeled, chopped and par-boiled
1 large flour tortilla

Directions:
1) In skillet over campfire, warm your sausage-potato mixture. Cook until potatoes are lightly browned. Add in lightly beaten eggs, scramble and cook. Remove from fire but keep warm.
2) Cut a 1-foot long foil and grease with oil.
3) On the greased part of oil, place flour tortilla. Add egg mixture in middle of tortilla. Add cheddar cheese, green onions and season with pepper and salt to taste.
4) Fold in one lower part of burrito. Fold in the right flap of burrito and roll to the other side. Wrap in greased foil and cook for 5 minutes per side or until cheese is melted and burrito is heated through.

Lumberjack Breakfast Foil Pack

Recipe below is good for two persons per foil pack.
Ingredients:
4 sausages
2 slices of bacon
2 eggs
2 cups hash browns
1 tomato, chopped
1 tbsp green onions, chopped
¼ cup shredded cheese
Pepper to taste
Directions:
1) In a 15-inch foil, grease and place in the middle 4 sausages. Place bacon slice son each side.
2) Top with hash browns, chopped tomato and eggs.
3) Add green onions and shredded cheese.
4) Sprinkle with pepper to taste and close foil sealing edges properly.
5) Place in a barbecue pit and cook for 15-20 minutes or until sausages are cooked.

Breakfast Potato Frittata

To make this easy for you, you can parboil potato at home and just keep in a zip lock bag inside your ice chest. You can also chop garlic, zucchini, peppers and onion ahead of time and store all in one zip lock bag.

Ingredients:
½ cup shredded cheddar cheese
1 clove garlic minced
1 small zucchini diced
½ red pepper, diced
½ green pepper, diced
1 medium onion, chopped
1 tbsps oil
Pepper to taste
½ tsp salt
½ tsp dried basil
½ cup milk
8 eggs
1 medium potato, peeled, diced and parboiled

Directions:
1) Heat a 10-inch cast iron skillet and add oil.
2) In a large bowl whisk together the eggs, pepper, salt, basil and milk.
3) In heated skillet, sauté the bag of onions and peppers for 3 minutes.
4) Add potatoes and continue sautéing for another 3 minutes.
5) Pour in egg mixture and cover top of skillet with foil. Allow to cook for 7 minutes.
6) Open foil, lift edge of egg to allow uncooked eggs to run underneath. Repeat on four other sides of the egg.
7) Drizzle cheese, return tin foil cover and cook for another 7 minutes or more or until eggs are set and cheese is melted.
8) Best served with a side of salad or bread.

Protein Rich Breakfast Muffin

All you need with this recipe is a muffin tin pan.
Ingredients:
1 Package bacon
12 slices whole grain bread
1 dozen eggs
Pepper and salt to taste
Directions:
1) Cut bacon in half and place 2-3 slices in bottom of each muffin hole. Try not to overlap the bacons.
2) Add one bread on top of the bacon pushing down to create a crater in the middle of the bread without breaking it.
3) Crack an egg and place directly on top of the bread crater.
4) Season with pepper and salt. Repeat the process until all muffin holes are filled.
5) Cover top with a sheet of foil and place on your campfire and cook for 10 minutes or until egg is cooked to desired doneness.

Chapter 2: Main Meal Camping Recipes

Quesadillas
This recipe yields 4 quesadillas.
Ingredients:
1 cup Shredded Mexican blend cheese
1 can black beans, rinsed and drained
1 jar Tostitos salsa con queso
2 8-oz chicken breasts, grilled and sliced
4 medium flour tortillas
Directions:
1) Place a tortilla on a flat surface and spread 1 tbsp of salsa on ½ of a side of the tortilla, leaving the other side bare. Place ¼ cup chicken over the salsa, top with ¼ cup black beans and ¼ cup cheese. Fold over the other half of tortilla to make a half moon.
2) Place quesadilla in a tin foil large enough to cover it completely. Repeat process for remaining ingredients.
3) Grill for 3-4 minutes per side or until cheese has melted and tortilla is crisped.

Foil Wrapped Herby Salmon

Ingredients:
Olive oil
¼ shallot, sliced
1 small garlic clove, minced
1 tbsp butter
1 sprig tarragon
1 sprig dill
1 tbsp Dijon mustard
2 slices lemon
1 salmon fillet
Directions:

1) In a foil packet large enough to accommodate salmon fillet, grease it with oil. Place salmon fillet with skin side down.
2) Add all herbs and season with pepper and salt. Place butter on top and lemon slice.
3) Drizzle with olive oil and seal foil well.
4) Place directly on fire or grill until salmon is cooked, around 6-8 minutes.

Nachos Pizza Style

I suggest you make the garlic cream sauce ahead of time in your kitchen and just place it in a bottle inside your cooler until time to be used.

Nachos Ingredients:
1 cup Colby Jack cheese, shredded
½ whole green bell pepper, seeds removed, diced
½ cups black olives sliced
½ cups Pepperoni, cut into bite sized pieces
¼ cups onion, diced
½ cups garlic cream sauce
Crispy tortilla chips

Garlic Cream Sauce Ingredients:
¼ cups Parmesan cheese, grated
1 pinch red pepper flakes
1 pinch cracked black pepper
1 pinch salt
¼ cup 2% milk
½ cup heavy cream
3 cloves garlic, minced
½ tbsps olive oil
1 ½ tbsp unsalted butter

Directions:
1) For the garlic cream sauce, place all ingredients in a food processor. Process until smooth and creamy. Transfer to a bottle and refrigerate until ready to be used.
2) During camping, in a cast iron skillet place as much tortilla chips as you can inside the skillet without overflowing.
3) Drizzle with garlic cream sauce. Add bell pepper, olive, pepperoni, onion and then cheese.
4) Grill until cheese is melted, around 10 to 20 minutes.

Balsamic Grilled Vegetables

Ingredients:
Black pepper to taste
Smoked Paprika to taste
Garlic salt to taste
1 tbsp Balsamic vinegar
2 tbsps Olive oil
6 garlic cloves, skin removed
1 red onion, cut into bite sized chunky pieces
8 oz cherry tomatoes
12 oz Green beans trim ends and cut in half
2 Portobello Mushrooms, cleaned and chopped into 1-inh pieces
Cheese and herbs for garnish, optional

Directions:
1) Cut 2 pieces of 15-inch long foil.
2) Place one foil on a flat surface and mix in all ingredients.
3) Cover with the other foil and seal edges properly
4) Place on top of a camp fire pit and grill for 8 minutes per side.
5) Remove from fire and allow to cool unopened for at least 5 minutes before enjoying.

Whole Wheat Pasta in Foil

The key here is to cook your whole wheat pasta ahead of time—at home. Then Pack them tightly into a zip lock bag, refrigerate in cooler until ready to use. The recipe below is good for 1 serving per packet

Ingredients:
1 tomato, cubed
1 tsp fresh basil
½ tsp garlic powder
Pepper and salt to taste
1 tbsp garlic pesto
2 tbsps goat cheese
1 cup whole wheat pasta

Directions:
1)In a foil packet, around 1-foot long. Place a cup of pasta. Add all ingredients with cheese on top.
2)Fold and seal foil packet.
3) Grill for 12 minutes and serve.

Barbecued Salmon

Ingredients:
½ tsp pepper
1 tsp salt
1 tbsp chopped fresh thyme leaves
2 tbsps Dijon mustard
¼ cup lemon juice
¼ cup dry white wine
¼ cup brown sugar
3 tbsps melted butter
3.5-4 lbs salmon fillet

Directions:
1) In small bowl, mix well pepper, salt thyme leaves, Dijon mustard, lemon juice, white wine, brown sugar, and melted butter.
2) Place salmon with skin side down on a foil and raise the sides of the foil to cover the sides of salmon.
3) Slather the mustard dressing mixture on top of salmon and grill for 25 to 30 minutes or until salmon is cooked yet still juicy.

Rice and Chicken Paella Style

Ready the following at home for easy campfire cooking: slice chorizo thinly and place in zip lock bag. Place olives in separate zip lock bag. Chop bell pepper and onions and place in a zip lock bag together. Into 3 pieces, evenly cut chicken thighs and season with ½ tsp paprika and salt. Place in zip lock bag and refrigerate all until ready to cook.

Ingredients:
8-oz shelled and deveined cooked small shrimp
1 14.5-oz can reduced sodium chicken broth
¾ cup Spanish fino sherry
2 cups Arborio rice
1 14.5-oz can diced tomatoes
¼ tsp saffron threads
3 large garlic cloves, minced
1 fennel bulb with feathery greens
3 tbsps olive oil, divided
2 ½ tsps smoked paprika, divided
1 ¼ tsps salt, divided
1 ½ lbs boned, skinned chicken thighs
½ lb Andouille sausage
1 cup pimiento stuffed green olives
1 green bell pepper

Directions:
1) On a 6 quart pot, heat oil. Add chorizo and for 5 minutes sauté until browned. With a slotted spoon, transfer to a plate.
2) In same pot, brown one side of chicken for 3-4 minutes per side. Turning over just once. If needed cook chicken in batches. Transfer cooked chicken to another plate.
3) Trim fennel and reserve feathery tops. Slice it lengthwise in half, remove core in a V and slice bulb thinly.
4) In same pot, heat remaining 2 tbsps of oil and sauté bell pepper, onions and sliced fennel for 7-8 minutes.

5) Add saffron, 2 tsps paprika, ¾ tsp salt and garlic. Sauté for a minute or two or until fragrant and sizzling.
6) Add tomatoes and continue sautéing for 5 minutes or until thick.
7) Add rice and stir to mix. Pour in chorizo, olives, broth, sherry and a cup of water. Cover and cook for 25 minutes or until liquid is absorbed and rice is tender.
8) Once rice is cooked, add shrimp, chicken and its juices on top of rice. Cover and cook for 5 minutes or until chicken and shrimp are heated through.
9) Chopped fennel fronds and top over chicken and shrimps and serve.

Camp Pizza

In order to make this successfully, you need to have a large cast iron skillet and charcoal briquettes for grilling.

Ingredients:
1 tbsp fresh oregano leaves
2 tbsps grated parmesan cheese
1 ½ cups coarsely shredded fontina cheese
½ cup store bought pizza sauce
1 tbsp fresh thyme leaves
¼ tsp pepper
¼ tsp salt
8-oz bulk Italian sausage
2 onions, halved lengthwise and thinly sliced
1 baked 10-inch pizza crust
3 tbsps olive oil

Directions:
1) Preheat a cast iron skillet on a charcoal grill. Grease skillet and once hot add pizza crust to toast for 5 minutes on one side. Remove from pan.
2) Add remaining oil to pan and sauté thyme, pepper, salt, sausage and onions for 10 minutes or until sausage are cooked and golden brown. Transfer to a plate.
3) Return pizza crust in pan with untoasted side facing down. Add pizza sauce on top and spread evenly. Add onion-sausage mixture and evenly spread.
4) Spread cheese evenly on top and cover skillet with foil.
5) Grill on low fire for at least 5-8 minutes checking bottom of crust to ensure it doesn't burn.

Pepper and Limed Grilled Chicken Breasts

You can marinate the chicken breasts while still at home and just remove from bag and ready to grill for an easy and delicious main meal recipe.

Ingredients:
4 boned, skinned chicken breast halves
1 tsp salt
1 tbsp olive oil
2 tbsps freshly ground black pepper
3 tbsps sugar
½ cup lime juice

Directions:
1) In a re-sealable bag mix ¼ cup water, salt, oil, pepper, sugar, and lime juice. Mix well until salt and sugar are dissolved.
2) With a mallet pound chicken breast until it is an even ¼-inch thick. Place inside re-sealable plastic with marinade and allow marinating for at least 30 minute or overnight.
3) Heat grill grate and once hot grill chicken breasts for 3-4 minutes per side.
4) Serve with bread or a side of salad.

Smoked Chili, Bacon and Beef Stew

Ingredients:
Shredded cheddar cheese, sliced green onions and sour cream – optional toppings
1 14.5-oz can pinto beans, drained
1 tsp Worcestershire
1 cup flavorful, medium-bodied beer such as Anchor Steam
1 8-oz can tomato sauce1 14.5-oz can crushed fire roasted tomatoes
1 tsp salt
1 tsp cayenne pepper
1 ½ tsps sweet smoked Spanish paprika
1 ½ tsps ground cumin
1 tbsp + 1 ½ tsp chili powder
1 ½ lbs lean ground beef
1 large garlic clove, minced

Directions:
1) Heat a heavy bottomed pot and pan fry bacon for 4 minutes until browned and crisped. Add onions and stir fry for 4 minutes or until soft and translucent. Add garlic and sauté for a minute.
2) Add ground beef and sauté until browned, around 10 minutes.
3) Add salt, pepper, paprika, cumin and chili powder. Continue sautéing for a minute.
4) Add Worcestershire, beer, tomato sauce and tomatoes. Cover and cook for 20 minutes or until simmering.
5) Add beans and continue cooking for another 10 minutes. Be sure to stir every once in a while.
6) Best served with toppings of sour cream, green onions and/or cheddar cheese.

Mushroom Campfire Foil Packet

Ingredients:
Pepper and salt to taste
3 tbsps extra virgin olive oil
2 tbsps fresh dill
2 garlic cloves, crushed
1 lb mixed mushrooms

Directions:
1) Line foil with parchment paper and grease with oil.
2) Add all ingredients, toss to mix and seal packet of foil properly.
3) Place on grill over campfire or coals and cook for 20 minutes.

Campfire Chicken Stew

Ingredients:
¼ tsp pepper
½ tsp salt
¼ cup water
1 can 10.75-oz condensed cream of mushroom soup
1 medium green pepper, sliced
1 cup thinly sliced carrots
4 medium potatoes, peeled and sliced
1 broiler chicken (3.5-4 lbs), cut up

Directions:
1) Grill chicken for three minutes per side as you preheat a pot.
2) Once chicken is done grilling, place all ingredients in pot including grilled chicken.
3) Cover and cook for 25 minutes or until chicken is cooked. If needed, continue cooking until desired doneness of chicken and veggies is reached.
4) Serve and enjoy.

Balsamic Steak

Ingredients:
A dash of cayenne pepper
Pepper and salt to taste
A dash of Worcestershire sauce
2 tbsps honey
1-2 tsps minced garlic
¼ cup olive oil
½ cup balsamic vinegar
1 lb top sirloin steak
4 potatoes

Directions:

1) In a zip lock bag, mix all ingredients and allow marinating for at least 4 hours, except for potatoes.
2) Wrap 1 potato in 2 layers of foil and place in fire as you grill steak for 5 minutes per side or to desired doneness. Remove potatoes from fire after 8 minutes.
3) Serve steak with a side of baked potatoes.

Cajun Shrimp Gumbo

Ingredients:
Corn starch
2 lbs shrimp
¼ cup chopped green onions
½ large can canned milk
Dash of cayenne pepper
¼ tsp pepper
1 tbsp sugar
1 can Rotel Diced Tomatoes & Green chilies
32-oz corn
¼ cup butter
2 cloves garlic, chopped
1 green pepper, chopped
1 onion, chopped

Directions:
1) Preheat a cast iron pot and heat butter. Once melted, add garlic, pepper and onions. Sauté until tender, around 3 minutes.
2) Add pepper, salt, sugar, tomatoes and corn. Cover and cook for ten minutes. Stir occasionally.
3) Add green onions and canned milk. Cover and cook for 5 minutes.
4) Add shrimp, cover and cook for 3 minutes.
5) Meanwhile, make a paste out of cornstarch and 2 tbsps water. Add into gumbo. Stirring continuously while cooking until sauce thickens.
6) Remove from fire, serve and enjoy.

Blue Cheese Burger Steaks

Ingredients:
2 tbsps Minute Maid frozen concentrated orange juice, thawed
¼ cup blue cheese, softened
1 tsp salt
1 tsp pepper
2 lbs ground beef
4 burger buns

Directions:
1) Mix well ground beef, salt and pepper. Divide into four and form 4 patties.
2) Grill burger patties to desired doneness, around 4 minutes per side.
3) Meanwhile, mix well orange juice and blue cheese until smooth and creamy.
4) After flipping the burgers once, spread the orange-blue cheese mixture over the top of each burger patties.
5) Grill the burger buns a minute per side.
6) Once patties are cooked, insert into burger buns and serve.

Chapter 3: Campfire Snack Recipes

Grilled Blueberry Cobbler

Ingredients:
1 can Pillsbury Buttermilk Biscuits
2 tbsps all-purpose flour
¼ cup granulated sugar
4 cups fresh blueberries (or raspberry, peaches, strawberry, etc.)
Directions:
1) Prepare your charcoals for grilling and start a fire.
2) As you wait for the fire to die down, in an 8-inch disposable baking dish mix flour and sugar. Add blueberries and cover top with foil.
3) Grill for 10 minutes, open, stir and close. Continue grilling until blueberries have released its juices, around 5-10 minutes more.
4) Add on top of blueberries the biscuits in a single file, cover with foil and continue grilling until biscuits are golden brown. Around 5-10 minutes.
5) Remove pan from grill, allow to cool for at least 5 minutes before serving.

Choco-Mallows in Banana Slit

Ingredients:
1 tsp miniature marshmallow
1 tsp semi-sweet Choco chips
1 medium banana unpeeled, ripe
Directions:
1) Make a slit on the banana lengthwise, ensuring not to slice all the way through. Do not peel banana and ensure to leave the peel on.
2) Insert the marshmallow and Choco chip inside the banana slit.

3) Wrap banana in foil, sealing the edges and grill for 7 minutes.
4) Remove from foil and enjoy.

Fruit & S'more Cones

Ingredients:
1 waffle ice-cream cone
1 tbsp semi-sweet chocolate chips
2 tbsps mini-marshmallows
¼ cup banana slices
¼ cup strawberry slices

Directions:
1) Place strawberry slices in waffle cone followed by banana, chocolate chips and marshmallows. Do not fill cone to the brim.
2) Wrap cone in foil and grill for 5-7 minutes.
3) Remove from fire; allow cooling a bit, peel off foil and enjoy.

Blueberry Muffin in Orange Balls

This is one of the most unique ways to enjoy blueberry muffins and a very special treat for your tots when camping. The beauty of this recipe is that you can prepare everything in the comfort of your home and just leave it near the fire pit to cook and after a quick dip; your muffins are waiting for you.

Ingredients:
1 box of blueberry muffin mix
6-8 large navel oranges

Directions:
1) Depending on the muffin mix you bought, you may need additional ingredients like milk, water, egg, butter or oil. So just follow the manufacturer's guide on making the blueberry muffin batter.

2)Slice oranges in half and scoop out the flesh and transfer to a bowl. You can use this flesh to make juice or store for future use as we won't need it in this recipe.

3) Fill the empty orange peel with blueberry muffin batter. Cover the blueberry muffin batter filled orange peel with an empty one wrap in 3 layers of foil. Repeat process for remaining oranges until all blueberry muffin batter is gone.

4)To cook, just toss these blueberry orange balls into the fire and leave them there for ten minutes or until they feel firm in the middle.

5)Unwrap and enjoy with a spoon or directly from the orange peel.

Orange-y Cinnamon Rolls

This snack recipe is perfect if you are looking for family fun filled way of making your own snack. It is easy and even kids can help and enjoy the activity of preparing their food.

Ingredients:
1 cinnamon rolls in a pop tube
6 oranges

Directions:
1)Slice cinnamon dough into 6-equal slices.

2)Cut oranges in half and scoop out flesh. You can eat the flesh or make it into orange juice.

3) For this recipe, what we will need are the intact orange peel and not the flesh. In one halved orange peel, place a slice of cinnamon dough and cover with the empty half of the orange peel. Wrap in 2 layers of foil. Repeat process to remaining dough and oranges.

4)To cook, just toss into fire and leave there for at least 8 minutes. If cooking on coals, it would take around 12 minutes, with flipping.

Hot Dog on Sticks with Bread

Ingredients:
1 package hotdogs
1 can refrigerated soft bread stick dough
Skewers

Directions:
1) Skewer hotdogs and wrap foil around exposed part of skewer.
2) Unroll bread sticks and separate in to strips. Wrap one strip of dough around each hotdog in a spiral fashion.
3) Cook hotdog over campfire while turning frequently until dough is golden brown and hotdog is cooked. You can also cooked on grill.

Pound Cake S'mores

Ingredients:
2 slices pound cake
Nutella spread
1 large marshmallow
Sliced fresh strawberries

Directions:
1) Slather 1 side of pound cake with Nutella.
2) Layer sliced strawberries over Nutella and top with a large marshmallow.
3) Cover marshmallow with the other slice of pound cake and wrap in foil.
4) Grill for 3 to 5 minutes or until marshmallow is melted.

Oreo S'mores

Ingredients:
1 Oreo cookie crushed
1 large marshmallow
1 chocolate graham cracker, broken in half
½ white chocolate bar

Directions:
1) On a foil place 1 chocolate graham cracker. Layer on the following in sequence: white chocolate bar, crushed Oreo cookie, marshmallow and the other graham cracker.

2) Wrap Oreo S'mores securely in foil and grill for 3-5 minutes or until marshmallow and white chocolate is melted.

It's OK to Have Some Fun

Go into a camping trip planning on being miserable the whole time and guess what? You're probably going to fulfill your prophecy. Go into the same camping trip with an open mind and you might find yourself actually having fun.

Yes, camping is dirty.

Yes, it can be very hot or very cold from time to time.

Yes, there are, YIKES, wild animals out and about.

Yes, there can be insects. Sometimes there are a lot of them.

No, you might not have electricity or running water.

And you know what? That doesn't stop millions of people spanning the entire globe from going camping and having a blast. If you think all there is to do while camping is sit in a hot, dusty campsite waiting for the trip to end, you've been going about camping all wrong. Camping trips should be fun for the entire family. The only thing required of you is that you're willing to try something new and go about it with an open mind.

For me, one of the biggest benefits of family camping trips is I get to get away with my family.

During the day, it's all about making sure the kids have a blast, and I have fun watching them have fun exploring nature and enjoying the many things the outdoors have to offer. Once the kids are down for the night, I get to spend quality time with my husband and any other adult family members or friends who came along on the trip. I also manage to squeeze a bit of alone time in, which I spend working on crossword puzzles, catching up on magazines I haven't had time to read at home or perusing a good book.

The rest of this chapter discusses just some of the things people do for fun while camping. Keep in mind that there are a lot of other things you can do, many of which are unique to the particular area where you're camping. Some campgrounds have full rec areas complete with miniature golf and pool tables. I've even stayed places that have full gyms, but working out is the last thing I want to do while I'm camping. I'm there to relax and distress, not to get my heart rate up, but that's just me.

Live a little and relax. It's OK to let yourself have fun while camping.

Go Hiking

Most campgrounds are close multiple trails that lead to scenic points and interesting vistas. When you get bored sitting around in your campsite, you can pass the time by exploring these trails either with your family in tow or without. You can often find everything from easy strolls around lakes and down rivers to grueling treks through dangerous mountain cutbacks within driving distance of a campsite—and sometimes they're part of the park you're camping in.

Hiking and exploring gives you the opportunity to get away from the paved roads and conveniences of society and allows you to experience nature much as our ancestors were able to experience it, with no white noise in the background and no throngs of tourists oohing and aahing. There's nothing more relaxing than hiking alone along a babbling brook in the mountains until you're deep into the woods and then stopping and enjoying the sounds of nature uninterrupted by the sound of passing vehicles and other people.

State parks, regional parks and national parks all usually have hiking trails, many of which lead you to solitary and beautiful areas rife with breathtaking scenery. If you're looking for some of the best sights known to man, you're going to have to be willing to hike in to many of them. The further you get from the pavement, the more likely you are to experience wildlife and nature as Mother Nature created it.

Deer, elk, mountain goats, bison, wolves, you name it. Depending on where you're hiking at, you might have a chance at lucking out and spotting one of these beautiful creatures.

My son and I went for a hike on a trail in Nevada recently and were walking along chatting it up when we came across a group of bighorn sheep. There were 5 of them in the group and when they saw us they slowly moved up the rocky outcropping they'd been grazing on. Three of the bighorn sheep had giant curved horns on their heads and they were a majestic site to see. We definitely wouldn't have seen them if we'd stayed put at the campground because they were extremely skittish around humans, but walking a couple miles up a nearby trail allowed us to get far enough away from camp to where we ran into them. We got some great pictures and now have a story to tell about the time we stumbled across the bighorn sheep.

Hiking is an enjoyable activity, but there are a few things you need to be aware of before you strike off into the wilderness.

Not all trails are created equal and some are created with the extreme hiker or backpacker in mind. Some trails through rough country amount to little more than a tiny path traversing dangerous cliffs and narrow switchbacks. While they can offer a good time for adventurous adults, you wouldn't want to bring your children anywhere near these trails. You also aren't going to want to strike off down one of these trails if you aren't in the best shape of your life—that is, unless you feel like getting airlifted off the mountain when you invariably find yourself in trouble.

It's a good idea to check trails out in advance by scouting them online, so you know whether they're family friendly. If you plan on having young children in tow, look for wide trails in relatively flat areas. The best trails for hiking with young children are typically found near waterways and lakes. If you still have questions or aren't able to find any kid-friendly trails in the area you're planning on staying, call a nearby ranger station. They're usually more than happy to point you in the right direction.

Create a plan detailing the path you plan on taking and map it out in advance. Setting off into the wilderness on an unknown course is a recipe for disaster. Trails can crisscross one another and there may be multiple forks in the trail along the way. Plan your route ahead of time and stick to it. Leave your plan with someone who isn't going hiking with you and let them know when you plan on being back, so if you don't return on time they'll know exactly where to start the search.

When creating a hiking plan, it helps to keep in mind the average person can hike 2 to 3 miles an hour under optimal conditions on flat land. If you have older people, people that are out of shape or children in the hiking party, it can be much less than that. It can also be much less than that if you're like me and want to stop and smell every flower along the way. If the trails are steep or are at a high altitude, that'll slow you down, too.

The longest trip most people are going to want to do in a single day is a 5 to 10 mile round trip and that's only if there are no young children along. Start your trips early in the day and you'll be able to enjoy the hike more than if you start in the afternoon and have to rush to get done before dark.

Keep in mind that it's the slowest member of your party that dictates the pace and plan accordingly. It doesn't matter how good of shape you're in if you have someone in tow who isn't in as good of shape. You're going to end up stopping and waiting on them, so plan your trip based on the shape the weakest member of your party is in.

Print out a map of the area you're hiking in and carry it and an ink pen or pencil with you. Each time you come to a fork in the trail, you can write it on your map, along with an identifying landmark or two. When it's time to head back to civilization, all you have to do is flip the map over and follow your trail back. Keep in mind that the way back is going to look different than the way there. Many a hiker has thought they were on the wrong trail because the way back looked so different they felt it couldn't possibly be the same path. Stop periodically and turn around and look at the way things are going to look on the way back. Identify landmarks you can use to make sure you're headed in the right direction and write them down.

Don't think for a second you can rely on GPS to get you home. Signals are notoriously spotty in remote areas and just because your GPS works at the trailhead, there's no guarantee it'll work once you're a mile or two in. Maps don't lose their signal, so always carry a paper map with you.

No matter what you do, always stay on the trail.

While it may be tempting to head off on your own to explore interesting photo ops and uncharted territory, this is also a great way to become hopelessly lost. If you do find yourself lost, don't attempt to find your way back to the trail. The whistle and flashlight you packed (you did pack a whistle and flashlight, right?) can be used to signal rescuers when you don't make it back to camp on time.

If you're a bit out of shape (or a lot, as I was before I started hiking regularly), the higher altitude trails are going to do a number on you. I remember my first camping trip to the mountains. I thought I was in pretty good shape because I'd been working out for a couple months preparing myself to hike to the top of Yosemite Falls in Yosemite National Park in California. The hike is a 7-mile round trip and I thought I was in pretty good shape because I'd hiked a 10-mile loop around a reservoir near my house a week earlier. Boy was I wrong. The elevation and the uphill stretches got to me and I was winded within the first mile. I had to stop every thirty seconds and rest in order to avoid passing out and tumbling off the side of the cliff. After the second mile, I started to sound like I was in an old war movie. I vaguely remember grabbing my husband and dramatically shouting something to the effect of, "I'm not going to make it. Just go on without me. I'll be here when you get back." He didn't leave my side, bless his soul, and I finally made it to the top of the falls. The view was breathtaking.

I begged my husband to call in a rescue chopper, but he refused. We finally made it back down the trail, a full 12 hours from the time we started.

Just because you're able to do something at a lower altitude doesn't mean you're going to be able to do the same thing at a higher altitude in the same amount of time. If you go hiking on trails in the mountains, be prepared to rest a lot and bring along plenty of water and food. That's actually good advice no matter where you're hiking. You never know how long you're going to be out and you don't want to get stranded somewhere with no food and water. While that mountain stream you've been following may look refreshing, you never know what it could be contaminated with. If you end up having to drink water of unknown quality from a natural source, you could get extremely sick. Harmful microorganisms are invisible to the naked eye and just because water looks clean doesn't mean it is.

There are a several items you should always carry with you when you're hiking:

A day pack to carry everything in. Invest in a lightweight and comfortable day pack with padded shoulder straps. If you're only planning on going on short hikes, a small day pack will suffice. If you're planning on doing longer hikes, an internal or external frame pack can help distribute the load of all of the stuff you're going to want to carry.

A compass. If you get lost, a compass can help you orient yourself. Make sure you learn how to use your compass before you need it.

A flashlight and extra batteries. Always carry a flashlight and extra batteries with you. If you get lost, the flashlight can be used to signal a rescue party.

Fire starter. You won't need this if everything goes according to plan. If not, you're going to be glad you have it. A lighter will usually suffice. You can pack a flint and striker if you know how to use one.

A map of the area and a pen or pencil. A trail map is one of the most important items to take with you when hiking. You can mark off the path you're taking and any forks in the road. You can also indicate landmarks you can use on the way back to help ensure you find your way.

A multitool. A multitool like a Leatherman can come in handy on the trail. It can be used to repair damaged gear and is great to have if you get lost.

A small first aid kit. Keep a small first aid kit in your bag that has antiseptic wipes, bandages, pain killers, sterile pads, tape and scissors in it, at a bare minimum. Be sure to pack any special medications you think you might need.

A whistle. This is another item that's good to have on hand in an emergency situation. Carry a loud whistle and you'll up your odds of being found quickly if you become lost.

Biodegradable toilet paper. This one's self-explanatory. Outhouses are few and far between on the trail and sometimes nature's call has to be answered, especially after a night of cocktails, s'mores and barbecue food. You don't want to have to wipe with leaves . . . trust me on this one.

Food (or at least snacks, if the hike will be a short one). Lightweight snacks that are high in calories like protein bars and trail mix are great for hiking food. Pack more than you think you're going to need. Hiking burns a lot of calories and you're going to be hungry. You don't want to get halfway through your hike and run out of snacks.

Plenty of water. Again, pack more than you think you're going to need. You're going to be thirsty. Really thirsty. Running out of water can really ruin a good time.

Sunscreen. Apply sunscreen liberally and then reapply it as needed. That is, unless you want to end up looking like a walking piece of beef jerky by the time you reach your golden years.

A jacket or heavy sweatshirt. Even if you plan on getting back long before the sun goes down, pack a jacket or heavy sweatshirt for each person in your group. The weather can change in an instant and you'll be glad you did if something happens and you end up out on the trail when the sun goes down.

A camera. You never know what you're going to come across on a hike. You're going to want to be able to take pictures.

A watch. It's all too easy to lose track of time on the trail. Carry a watch with you so you'll know when it's time to turn around and head back.

Wear comfortable clothing and invest in a nice pair of light trail shoes or hiking boots—and be sure to break them in before setting off on a long hike. New shoes can be extremely uncomfortable until they're broken in and blisters are all-too-common on the trail. Broken-in shoes that fit well and good socks can go a long way toward alleviating blisters (and foot pain in general).

Start off slow and pick hikes that are within your limitations. Attempting to hike to the top of Half Dome on your first hiking trip is asking for disappointment—and maybe quite a bit of pain and suffering. For those who don't know, Half Dome is a strenuous 14+ mile hike to the top of a large rock in Yosemite Park in California. At the end of the hike, you have to traverse up the infamous cable section, using cables to climb your way up the steep rock face to the top of the Dome. If you're going to attempt a hike like this on your first attempt at hiking, take out a good life insurance policy ahead of time.

Hiking and exploring trails is a great way to have fun, as long as you hike safely and don't try to do too much. Know your limitations and plan hiking trips everyone in your group will be able to enjoy.

Just to review, here are the safety rules you should follow before and during a hiking trip:

Before the Trip

Make sure you're physically fit enough to handle the hiking trip you're planning.

Plan your route.

Print out or purchase a trail map of the area.

Let a friend or family member know where you're going and when you plan on returning.

Pack the gear mentioned earlier in this chapter. Make sure it's all in good working order.

During the Trip

Watch your step.

Stay on the trail.

Be prepared for inclement weather.

Don't try to cross a stream that's flowing too fast to safely traverse. Some trails will be blocked by fast-running water in the spring or during unexpected storms.

Keep a close eye on the kids. Don't hike trails that are beyond their skill level. You don't want to end up carrying an exhausted child while walking a trail.

Don't deviate from your chosen path.

Always check footholds and handholds before placing your weight on them. If you slip, you could end up taking everyone below you out as you go.

Don't overestimate your abilities.

Stop and look behind you periodically. You'll be surprised how different things look going in the opposite direction.

What to Do If You're Lost

It's unlikely to happen if you're careful and stick to the planned route, but there's a slight chance you could find yourself off the trail and unable to find it—or on an unfamiliar trail that leads into the unknown. Make sure you and everyone in your party is well-versed on what to do if they get lost, especially any children you have with you. Every person in your party should have their own food, water, whistle and flashlight. That way, if they get separated from the group, they'll be able to alert the rest of the party immediately. If they're separated for any period of time, having their own water and food could save their life.

Here's what you need to do if you get lost:
- As soon as the lost person realizes they're separated from the group, the person should stop and stay in place. Continuing to walk could move them further in the wrong direction. The closer they are to the trail, the faster they'll be found.
- Start blowing the whistle immediately. Chances are the rest of the group will still be close enough to hear you. If you're hiking alone, blow the whistle once every few minutes and listen for a response. If you hear a response, continue blowing the whistle until you're found.
- Adults in the group can pick a landmark in the area where they're lost and can walk a distance from the landmark, keeping it in sight while looking for the trail. They can then walk back to the landmark and try again in a different direction. Having a compass on-hand and knowing how to use it can help you head in the right direction. If you aren't sure, you're probably better off waiting where you are, unless you're in danger of starving or dying of dehydration.
- Don't rush. If you panic and rush off, you're more likely to find yourself hopelessly lost.
- Stay close to an open area. If you're lost and are hunkered down in a thick stand of trees, you're a lot less likely to be found than you are if you're in an open area. If you don't want to be exposed to the elements, use rocks to create an S.O.S. message and an arrow pointing to where you're at.
- A fire can be used to create a smoke signal by day and a flame to guide rescuers at night. Make sure you clear a wide enough area around your fire to where you won't start a forest fire. That's the last thing you need when lost in the wilderness.

It helps to keep in mind the vast majority of hikers never find themselves in trouble. Carrying safety gear that you know how to use and keeping trail safety in mind will ensure you aren't part of the unfortunate minority. Many of the hikers who find themselves in big trouble end up that way because they don't know how to safely hike and follow trails.

A little education goes a long way.

Hit the Water

Rare is the campsite that doesn't have some type of water nearby. Rivers, lakes, ponds and swimming pools all offer unique activities you can partake in to stave off boredom. There are literally thousands of things you can do in, around and on bodies of water.

The following are some of the more common water-related activities:

Boating

If you have a boat, you're probably no stranger to the long list of activities a boat opens up to you. You can find a quiet cove away from the crowded areas those without boats frequent where you can hang out and swim, fish or just relax for as long as you'd like.

You can explore the body of water you're on, looking for something that piques your interest. You can also go skiing, tubing or wakeboarding, which are more strenuous, but are good ways to keep older kids and teenagers entertained.

No boat? No problem—many of the larger lakes and waterways have places you can rent a boat from.

Diving and Snorkeling

Tired of being above the water? Get below it by taking a diving or snorkeling trip. In a clear body of water, you'll be amazed by the vegetation and sea life there is swimming below the surface.

Fishing

If you're near a body of water that's been around for a while and is at least a few feet deep, there's a pretty good chance there's fish in it.

New bodies of water can be tough to fish.

Bring your children with you to a local tackle shop and ask for help. Locals are much more likely to divulge information to a woman with children in tow, so ladies, this one's up to you. You never know . . . the tips you get may help the kids catch dinner.

Be sure to check with your local fish and game agency to see if there are heavy metals or other contaminants in the water. You don't want to eat the fish if there are.

Float around

Procure something that floats. Anything big enough to hold you afloat will work. A raft, a life vest, an inner tube, etc. Hop in the water and float around for a while. Be careful you don't float too far out to sea or you're going to have a tough time getting back.

If you do find yourself stranded, as I'm embarrassed to admit I once did when I fell asleep, flag down a passing boat. They'll get a kick out of your story and should be willing to return you to shore.

Rafting

If there's a river with a decent current nearby, floating down it in a raft can be a ton of fun. Some rivers are slow enough to enjoy in an inner tube, while others require large rafts and aren't for the faint of heart.

Skipping rocks

Want a quick detour to the water to distract bored kids?

Find a body of water—pretty much any body of water will do—and teach your kids to skip rocks. Flat rocks work best. Throw the rock so it hits the water and the flat side skims across the water. Skilled stone skippers can get a rock to skip 20 or more times before it sinks below the surface. How many times can you get a rock to skip? We keep records for the day, the trip and there's an all-time record of 10 skips set by my husband that no one else in the family has yet come close to.

Swimming

Find a lake, pond or swimming pool and hop in. Kids love to spend hours swimming. Be sure to slather on copious amounts of sunscreen and don't forget to reapply regularly. You don't want to cope with nasty sunburns later on when you get back to camp. Find a place where other children are swimming and your kids will have even more fun.

Sports and Recreational Games

Get off your butt and get active.

There are all sorts of sports and recreational games you can engage in while camping. It's as easy as bringing a ball or some gear and finding a good spot. Here are a handful of ideas to get you started:

Baseball

As long as you have room to pack the gear, baseball (or softball, for that matter) can be a fun way to pass time. Don't have room for all the gear? A broomstick and a couple tennis balls can be just as much fun.

Bike riding

You can buy a bike rack that allows you to attach bicycles to the back of your vehicle or you can call ahead and find a place that rents bicycles by the day. Some campsites have bikes available for a nominal fee.

Capture the flag

While your kids may have played the video game version of capture the flag in popular video games like Halo and Call of Duty, they probably haven't played the real-life game it's based on.

Two groups of kids are split up into teams, each of which has a flag. The goal of the game is to sneak into the opposing team's base and grab their flag without getting tagged out. When a player gets tagged on the opposing team's side, the player has to return to their base for a designated amount of time before heading out again. The winner is the first team to capture the opposing team's flag and return it to their base without getting caught.

Corn hole

Also called bean bag toss and baggo, to play corn hole all you need are 8 bean bags and 2 flat surfaces that are 2 feet by 4 feet with a 6" hole centered 9 inches down from the top of the platforms. The back end of the platforms should be raised a foot off the ground, leaving the platform sitting at an angle. Separate the platforms so there is 27 feet between the bottom edges of the platform.

Here are the rules of the game:
- Play is divided into innings, in which each player throws 4 bean bags.
- Players must stand behind the bottom edge of one of the platforms and throw at the other platform. Crossing in front of the bottom edge is a foul and no points are scored for the toss. Players can stand on one side of the platform or the other, but all throws by a player in a single inning must be from the same side.
- Bags thrown through the hole are worth 3 points.
- Bags that land on and stay on the board until the end of the inning are worth 1 point. Bags that touch the ground first and bounce onto the board aren't scored.
- If a player from one team lands a bag in the hole and it's followed up by a hole shot from the other player, the shots cancel each other out and no points are scored.
- The game is won by the first player or team to reach 21 points.

Disc golf

I don't know whether this holds true nationwide, but a number of campgrounds and parks in my area have disc golf courses set up that can be used for free or for a nominal fee.

The game is played similar to golf, but you use a Frisbee instead of a club and balls. The goal is to get the Frisbee into the basket in as few throws as possible.

Don't have a course near you? Not a problem. An empty garbage can makes a great basket and can be moved around to create different "holes" to play.

Football

Whether playing a full-on flag football game, two-hand touch or just tossing a ball around, football can be a great way to pass time while camping.

Hide and Seek

Here's an oldie, but goody.

Hide and seek is a time-honored game that kids nowadays rarely play. A base is chosen at the start of the game. One person is it and counts to a predetermined number while the rest of the players hide. When the person who is it finished counting, he or she sets off looking for the hidden players. Players try to make it back to a designated base before they're caught by the it person. The last person caught gets to choose who is it for the next game.

Horseshoes

Tossing horseshoes at a peg may not sound like fun, but it's actually a great way to pass the time.

Here's a quick and easy rundown of the rules to get you started:

- Games are either played until someone reaches 40 points or there are 40 shoes thrown by each person. Your call.
- Each player gets two horseshoes to pitch. One player pitches his horseshoes, and they're followed by the next player's horseshoes.
- Shoes have to be within a horseshoe's width of the stake to be scored.
- The closest horseshoe to the stake scores one point in each round. If both of your shoes are closer than your opponent's, you get 2 points.
- Ringers occur when the horseshoe encircles the stake. If you place a straight edge across the gap in the horseshoe and it touches the stake, it doesn't count as a ringer. Ringers are worth 3 points. A ringer is cancelled if another player throws a ringer on top of it.
- If you have a ringer and the closest horseshoe in a round, you get 4 points.

- Leaners are shoes that are leaning against the stake. They count as one point. Ringers are considered closer to the stake than leaners when considering who gets the points for the closest stake.

Ladder toss

This game is played by throwing bolas, which are 2 balls connected by strings, at a PVC pipe ladder that has 3 rungs. The top ladder is worth 1 point, the middle ladder 2 and the bottom ladder 3. Having a bola on each rung is worth 10 points. Most games are played to 21 points and some variations of the game reverse the scoring, so the top rung is worth 3.

Lawn bowling

In this game, players roll 4 bowls in an attempt to get them the closest to a smaller white ball, known as a jack. Points are scored for each bowl the player has that's closer to the jack than the other player's bowls.

Rock climbing

Inexperienced climbers should take lessons before attempting to climb on their own. Rock climbing is a fun, albeit rather demanding, way to kill time. It isn't for the faint of heart, but those in good shape with an adventurous side will love this pastime.

Soccer

Grab a soccer ball and set up a couple cones as goals and you've got a makeshift soccer goal that can be used for pickup games and shooting practice.

Spelunking

Hire a guide and go exploring local caves. You'll be amazed by some of the stuff you find underground. Stalactites, stalagmites and all sorts of other interesting rock formations can be found deep beneath the surface of the earth.

Tag

Tag is a playground games that can be played while camping. It involves one player or a team of players chasing other players in an attempt to tag them. When an opposing player is tagged, they either become "it" or are out of the game until the next round.

There are a number of variations on the game of tag. Here are some of the more popular versions of tag:

- Ball tag. The "it" person uses a ball to tag opposing players, either by rolling it at them or throwing it at them. Make sure you use soft balls for this game.
- British Bulldog. This game is played in a rectangular play area. Two players start in the middle and all the other players start at one end of the play area. The goal is for the players to run to the other end without being tagged by the players in the middle.
- Chain tag. When a player is tagged they have to hold hands with the "it" player, creating a chain of players that has to work together to run other players down. The players at the end of the chain are the only ones who can tag someone out because they're the only ones with a free hand.
- Elimination tag. The tagged players are out of the game. The game ends when the "it" person has tagged everyone out. The last person to be tagged out in the game chooses the "it" person for the next round.
- Flashlight tag. This game is played at night and players attempt to tag other players using the beams of light emitted from a flashlight.
- Freeze tag. Tagged players are frozen in place and must stay where they are until they're tagged by a player who isn't it.
- Bomb's away. The "it" player throws a soft ball as high as he or she can in the air. As soon as the ball is thrown, all players take off away from the "it" person. When he or she catches the ball and shouts "Bomb's away!" all of the other players have to stop. The "it" player is then allowed to take 2 large steps toward any player they'd like. If they then throw the ball and hit the player, that player is out of the game. They can then start from where that player is and take two more steps toward any other player on the field. If they throw the

ball and hit that player, that player is out. The game continues until the "it" person has hit all of the players in the game or has missed with three throws.
- Shadow tag. Players try to step on the shadow of other players to tag them out. In my experience, this game results in a lot of arguing about whether or not a person's shadow was indeed stepped on.
- Zombie tag. One person starts off as a zombie and everyone else is human. As the zombie tags other players, they become zombies as well. The game continues until one person is left. That person wins the game and starts the next game as the zombie.
- Wood tag. Players are considered safe and can't be tagged out when touching something made of wood.

Washers

The rules vary depending on where in the nation you're playing washers, but the basic premise is the same. Toss washers into a cup to score points.

1" washers are the washers of choice and the cups are set into a platform or dug into the ground so they're level with the surface around them. Paint them different colors in groups of 4, so you'll be able to tell them apart during a game.

Here's a general scoring system you can use to play the game of washers:
- Washers that land in the cup are worth 5 points. If a player throws a washer in the cup after an opposing player lands a washer in it, the score is cancelled out and neither player scores.
- A hanger is a washer that hangs over the edge of the cup, but doesn't fall in. These are worth 2 points if the hole in the washer doesn't extend over the edge of the cup and 3 if it does.
- If no one gets a washer in the cup or a hanger, the player with the washer closest to the cup is awarded one point.

- The winner is the first person or team to reach or pass 21 points.

Card Games

Not into activities that are physically exerting? Don't worry; you don't have to sit around bored. Card games are a great way to pass time without ever having to leave the campsite. They're a fun way to wrap up a long day and wind down before bed.

Get out a deck of cards and gather around the campfire. These games are fun for the whole family and easy enough that all but the smallest members of the family should be able to join in.

Go Fish

Players: 3 to 6

Supplies needed: 1 deck of cards

Rules:

Shuffle the deck and deal 5 cards to each player. Place the remaining cards face down in a draw pile. The goal of the game is to collect sets of 4 cards that are the same rank.

The first player picks one of the other players and asks for a card. The player asking for the card has to have at least one of the cards they're asking for in their deck. If the player has the card being requested, they have to give it to the requestor. The requestor then gets to continue his or her turn and can ask the same player or another player for a card.

If the player doesn't have the card being requested, the player says "go fish" and the requestor has to draw the top card from the draw pile. If it's the card the player requested, the player shows it to the group and gets to continue his or her turn. If not, the player's turn is over and play is passed to the person to the left of the player.

When a set of four cards of the same rank is collected, the player holding the cards reveals the cards to the group and then places them face down in a pile in front of themselves.

Play continues until the draw pile runs out or one of the players has no cards left in their hand. The player with the most sets of cards at this time is declared the winner.

Liar

Players: At least 3

Supplies needed: 1 to 2 decks of cards

Rules:

Shuffle the deck of cards and deal the cards until all cards have been dealt. The goal of the game is to be the first player to get rid of all of the cards being held.

To get rid of cards, you place a number of cards of the same type face down in the middle of the table and announce what they are. For example, you could place 4 jacks in the middle and announce "4 jacks." You're allowed to lie about what you're placing on the table. You could place 2 jacks and 2 queens face down on the table and announce "4 jacks."

Once the cards are placed on the table, the other players have the opportunity to accuse the player of lying by announcing "Liar." If no one accuses the player of lying, the cards are left face down and put in the discard pile. If someone announces "Liar," the cards are flipped over to check and see if the player is lying or not. If the player is caught lying, the "Liar" must take all of the cards in the discard pile. If the person told the truth about what was being discarded, the accuser must take all of the cards in the discard pile.

The game continues until all of the players except one have gotten rid of their cards. The winner is the first person to get rid of his or her cards.

Old Maid

Players: 3 to 8

Supplies needed: A deck of cards, with three of the queens removed from the deck.

Rules:

The one queen left in the deck is the Old Maid. The goal is to be one of the players that aren't holding the Old Maid at the end of the game.

A designated dealer should shuffle the deck and deal the cards evenly to the group. If some players have more cards than others, it's OK. Once all of the cards have been dealt, players look at their cards and place any pairs they find face down in front of them.

The dealer allows the player to his left to draw one card. If a matching pair is made, the player discards the pair. If not, the player adds the card to his or her hand and keeps it. This player then allows the player to his or her left to draw a card and do the same.

Play continues around the circle until the only card left is the Old Maid. The player holding the Old Maid at the end of the game loses the game.

Slap Jack

Players: 2 to 5

Supplies needed: 1 deck of cards

Rules:

Deal all of the cards to the players. It doesn't matter if players have uneven numbers of cards. The cards are placed face-down in a pile in front of each player.

The player to the left of the dealer flips the top card on his pile over and places it in the center of the play area. If it's any card other than a Jack, play continues on to the next player. If the card is a Jack, the first person to slap their hand over the Jack is the winner of the pile of cards in the middle.

Once a player loses all of his or her cards, that player is out of the game. That is, unless he's able to slap the next Jack that's laid down. Out players can only slap the next Jack laid down after they run out of cards. After that, they're permanently out. The last person left in the game is declared the winner.

Spoons

Players: 3 to 7

Supplies needed: 3 decks of cards and spoons. The number of spoons will be equal to the total number of players minus one. For example, a game with 5 players would use 4 spoons.

Rules:

Play this game by circling your chairs around a central location to which each player has equal access. Place the spoons in the middle of the play area. The handles of the spoons should be facing outward.

Four cards should be dealt to each player. The player is allowed to pick these cards up and look at them. The rest of the cards are dealt face-down to each player. Each player goes in a circle and draws a card from their pile and adds it to their hand. If a player gets 4 of a kind, the player reaches out and grabs a spoon. As soon as the other players see the player reach for a spoon, they can all try to grab a spoon as well. The player left without a spoon is out of the game.

Remove one spoon from the play area and continue the game until all but one player has been eliminated.

A variant of this game has the dealer deal 4 cards to each player and then place the deck next to him. He then draws the top card from the deck and either keeps it or discards it by placing it in front of the player to the left of him. If he discards a card, he must draw another card from the top of the deck and keep it. If the dealer keeps the first card, he must draw the top card and place it in front of the player next to him without looking at it.

Play continues to the player the dealer passed the card to. The player checks the card in front of him and either passes it and draws a new card or keeps the card and places a new card in front of the player to his left. This continues around the circle until someone gets 4 of a kind and reaches for a spoon. Everyone tries to grab a spoon and the person without a spoon is eliminated, their cards are added to the bottom of the deck and play continues around the circle until all but one player has been eliminated.

UNO

Uno is a fun game that requires a special deck of UNO cards to play. The rules can get a bit complicated, but each deck of UNO cards comes complete with the rules. Up to 10 players are able to play at once using a single deck. Because of the number of players that can play, this is a good game for large groups of people.

War

Players: 2

Supplies needed: 1 deck of cards.

Rules:

Shuffle the deck and deal the cards evenly between the two players. Each player should place the cards face down in front of them without looking at them.

The players take the top card off of the deck and flip it over. The player holding the card with the highest face value wins the round and gets to keep both cards. Here's the face value order of the cards, from highest to lowest:

- Ace
- King
- Queen
- Jack
- 10
- 9
- 8
- 7
- 6
- 5
- 4
- 3
- 2

If two cards with the same face value are played, War is declared. Each player states "I declare War" while laying down a card with each syllable of the statement. The 4th card is placed faced up and the winner is the player with the card with the highest face value. If the face value is a tie again, another War is declared. The winner of any War wins all of the cards in the pile.

The player to take the entire deck of cards is the winner. Alternatively, the person with the most cards after a set frame of time or a certain number of Wars is declared the winner.

Cooking While Camping

I don't know whether it's because the days are spent running around and having fun and you return to camp tired and hungry, but there's nothing as good as eating a well-cooked dinner by the light of a campfire. Camp food tastes great, is filling and cooking and eating around the campfire is a good way to wrap up a great day.

Cooking food over a campfire allows you to experience mealtime much in the same manner the pioneers experienced it when first exploring the nation. Some campers bring along a barbecue and a camp stove as well. I use a camp stove from time to time, but the barbecue is left at home. Any grilling or barbecuing is done on a grate placed over the campfire.

The downside to cooking in camp is it's much slower than cooking at home. You have to be patient and willing to improvise when it comes to cooking techniques and food preparation. Set aside plenty of time for cooking meals because you're going to need it.

There are a number of methods you can use to cook while camping. The following methods are some of the more common methods.

Camp Stoves

Bring along a camp stove and you'll be able to cook in a manner similar to the way you'd cook on a gas stove at home. A double-burner camp stove will give you two burners you can use at the same time to speed up the cooking process.

Push-button ignition stoves are the easiest because all you have to do is press a button and the stove lights itself. At least they work that way the first few times you light them. Once they age a bit, they tend to require multiple pushes of the button until the stars align correctly and the stove finally lights. My husband typically ends up using a lighter or matches to light our fancy push button stoves because it's easier and less frustrating.

Lightweight stoves are available that are geared toward backpackers, but this isn't a necessity for the weekend camper. If you plan on backpacking, a small single-burner stove is a good option.

Liquid gas stoves burn fuels like kerosene or white gas. They have refillable gas tanks designed to hold a number of different fuel types. The tanks are usually detachable, so you only have to take the tank in to get it filled. These stoves are bulky and heavy, but they burn hotter and have adjustable flames that can be used in most weather conditions.

Cartridge stoves are less expensive and lighter than liquid gas stoves, but they aren't as durable as their bulkier counterparts. They use gas cartridges filled with gases like propane or butane. The cartridges are one-time use items that are thrown away once they're empty. These stoves burn clean and are easier to use than liquid gas stoves, except for when the wind picks up or the weather cools down to below 35 degrees F, at which time they're tough to keep lit. You can purchase a heat exchanger that'll allow you to use your stove in cooler temperatures.

Cartridge stoves are a good choice if you're concerned with weight because the cartridges are light and some cartridges can be used to light both lanterns and cartridge stoves. If weight and space isn't of concern, you're better off going with a liquid gas stove.

Camp stoves are rated by their efficiency, which is the amount of time it takes for the stove to completely deplete a full fuel canister or tank when turned all the way up, and boil time, which is the amount of time it takes for the stove to bring one quart of water to a boil at sea level when the air temperature is 70 degrees F and the stove is turned all the way up. The efficiency of the stove isn't much of a concern as long as you bring along enough fuel to last you the entire trip. The boil time indicates how hot the stove burns. Lower boil times mean it's going to take a longer time to cook your food.

You could spend a lot of money on the latest and greatest technology in camp stoves, but that really isn't necessary. Walk around any campground and you're likely to find most campers have a 2-burner propane camp stove, usually made by Coleman. Save yourself some cash and buy a Coleman camp stove, which won't break the bank and is the brand of choice for many happy campers across the nation. They cost less than a hundred bucks and will make short work of breakfast, coffee and pretty much any other cooking task you'd want to engage in while camping.

There's no real need to get too fancy with your cook stove. As long as you have a flame and stable place to set your stove, you should be good to go.

Charcoal Barbecues

You can bring a charcoal barbecue along with you or you can bring a grate and use a fire ring with charcoal. If you've barbecued at home with charcoal, you already know how to use a charcoal barbecue. You can get a similar effect by lighting a wood fire and letting the wood burn down until there are nothing but hot coals left.

Here's a quick primer on getting charcoal started:
1. Clear the grill of ash and dirt before starting it.
2. Remove the grate from the grill.
3. If there are vents on the bottom of the grill, set them to the open position.
4. Arrange the briquettes in a pyramid at the bottom of the grill.
5. Add lighter fluid to the briquettes and let it soak in.
6. Light the briquettes using a long lighter or a match. Don't stand too close to the grill because it can light up quickly if you used a lot of lighter fluid.
7. If the grill is dirty from being previously used, put the grill back on while the flame is burning and let the heat burn the

grease and grime off of the grill. Scrape it with a wire brush once the flames go down.
8. Let the charcoal burn until the coals are covered with a light coating of thin ash and are glowing red.
9. Spread the charcoal out and place any half-lit pieces between coals that are completely lit and burning red. Don't add more lighter fluid. This will make the food taste like lighter fluid and may put out the lit charcoals.
10. You're ready to cook. Get to it.

Briquettes are available that claim not to need lighter fluid, but I've found they're hit and miss. The brand name self-igniting briquettes work well, but the cheaper brands won't stay lit. It's up to you whether you want to pay extra for the self-lighting briquettes.

The Charcoal Chimney

A charcoal chimney can be used to ensure briquettes light without use of lighter fluid.

The typical charcoal chimney is a metal cylinder into which briquettes are place. The briquettes at the bottom of the chimney are lit using newspaper or starter cubes and the coals burn evenly from the bottom up. The chimney helps the coals light up faster and they'll be ready to cook on in a shorter amount of time. When the coals are ready, dump them into the barbecue or fire pit you're ready to cook.

Here's a pro tip to help you get your coals started right. When you add newspaper to the bottom, crumple it lightly and add a bit of cooking oil to the newspaper. More air equals more oxygen for the fire and the cooking oil will help get the newspaper lit and keep it burning long enough to light up your coals.

Charcoal Grilling Tips

The following tips should help you successfully grill food on a charcoal barbecue:

- Don't constantly turn your food or you run the risk of drying it out. Ideally, you want to cook it completely on one side before flipping and cooking the other side.
- Don't pack your food too tightly onto the grill. You want to leave air space around your food in order to allow it to cook evenly.
- Lighter cubes can be used to light charcoal. Place a lighter cube beneath the charcoal pyramid and light the cube. The charcoal will then light from the bottom up.
- Sauces with sugar in them will burn easily. Don't put them on until you're almost done with the meat.
- Spray non-stick cooking spray on your grill to keep food from sticking to it.
- Use a spray bottle with water in it to knock down any flames that rise up because of grease hitting the coals. Flames are problematic because they char your meat and cause it to cook unevenly.

Direct and Indirect Grilling

Direct grilling is a cooking process in which the meat is placed on the grill directly over the hot coals. It's the method most people use for barbecuing. Direct grilling is the best method of grilling for sausages, individual pieces of chicken, steak, pork chops and ground meat.

Indirect grilling places the food you're cooking on the grill so it isn't placed directly above the coals. The coals are on one side of the grill and the meat is placed on the grate on the other side. Food cooks more slowly with the indirect grilling, which is recommended for larger foods like whole birds, ribs and tough meats like brisket and pork shoulder. It can also be used to grill delicate foods like certain types of fish that would be destroyed by direct heat.

When indirect grilling is used, most meats benefit from a quick five or six minute searing. To sear meat and lock in the flavor, place it over direct heat for 2 to 3 minutes on each side. It'll cook the outside of the meat, leaving the inside soft and tender. Move it to indirect heat to finish the cooking process.

Wood Fire

Cooking over a wood fire is one of my favorite ways to cook up a camp meal. Food can be cooked on a grill over a wood fire or you can use pots and pans to cook up a wide variety of foods. Your campfire can be used to cook breakfast, lunch and dinner as long as you keep it going and periodically add wood to keep it hot.

The best part about using a wood fire is the smoky, woody flavor it imparts to the food. The flavor of your food largely depends on the type of wood used to build the fire. Oak, applewoods, nut woods and a number of other woods can be used, and all impart a unique flavor to the foods that are cooked over them. Avoid woods like pine that impart a bitter taste to food.

The following woods are popular choices for cooking over:

- Alder.
- Apple.
- Cedar.
- Cherry.
- Hickory.
- Maple.
- Mesquite.
- Nut woods.
- Oak.

An adjustable cast-iron grill that sits on legs that rest on both sides of the grill will make life much easier if you plan on cooking over your campfire. Meats can be grilled directly on the grill and pots and pans can be placed onto the grill for foods you don't want to cook over an open flame. Adjustable grills can be moved up and down, so you're able to control how close your food is to the fire.

If you really want to go all out, invest in a Dutch oven or a cauldron that can be placed directly into the fire. Make sure you read up on how to properly season a Dutch oven before use.

Using one of these allows you to slowly cook up a number of delicious soups and stews. You haven't lived until you've had clam chowder made from clams you just caught at the beach and cooked up in a Dutch oven.

Campfire Cooking Tips

The following tips will help you successfully cook over a campfire:

- Dry, seasoned woods are best for campfire cooking. They make hotter burning fires with less smoke, which is what you ideally want to cook over.
- You don't have to wait for the fire to burn all the way down to cook over a wood fire. In fact, small flames can be used to sear meat and add extra flavor to it. If flare-ups occur, you can move your meat away from the flare-ups to another area of the grill.
- Set aside plenty of time for building the campfire and getting it to a point where it's ready to be cooked over. It can take as long as a couple hours for logs to be reduced to coals that are easy to cook over.
- You can practice indirect cooking with wood fires. Let the wood burn down to coals with no flames. Move the coals to one side of the fire pit and place the food you want to indirectly cook on the other side.

The Campfire: An Age-Old Tradition

The campfire is an age-old tradition that has probably been around since man invented fire. It's definitely been around for hundreds, if not thousands or millions, of years. I can picture Grug the caveman sitting around a campfire bragging to other cavemen about the mammoth that got away. Fast forward a million or so years to last few centuries and our forefathers sat around campfires for warmth and used them to cook food and warm coffee much in the same way we do today.

If you've never built a campfire before, the first time you try to build one can be an exercise in frustration, especially if you're

trying to build a fire on a windy day. Let's take a look at the steps involved in building a campfire:
1. If you're lucky, the campsite will already have a fire ring or fire pit. If it does, use the already made ring or pit. Skip ahead to step 5. If not, you're going to have to build a fire ring or pit yourself.
2. Clear the area around where you're going to build your campfire ring. You don't want a loose ember to be able to get away and start a fire. Remove all organic material and anything flammable from an area that's at least 10 feet in all directions from the location where you plan on building the fire.
3. You can dig a fire pit if you want. Some camp areas require use of a fire pit. Dig the pit to 6" to 12" deep and 2 to 4 feet wide. A fire pit will provide an added layer of protection from the wind.
4. Gather dry rocks and use them to build a circle around your fire pit. Wet rocks should not be used, as they can explode when heated. Fit the rocks together as tightly as you can. The rock also provides protection from the wind. Stack the rocks until the ring is at least a foot tall and fill in any gaps with smaller rocks or gravel.
5. Now that you've got your fire ring built, it's time to build your campfire. Gather tinder, which consists of small twigs and dry grass and leaves, and kindling, which are small sticks. You're also going to need larger pieces of wood to burn in your fire.
6. Pile a couple handfuls of tinder in the center of the fire ring.
7. Crisscross the smaller kindling over the tinder.
8. Light the tinder. It should flare up and start to ignite the kindling.
9. Blow gently on the tinder to help stoke the flame. If necessary, light the tinder in a handful of places.

10. As the kindling catches fire, add more kindling to get a good fire going. Begin adding larger pieces of wood one at a time until you get the fire going.
11. Keep the fire going by adding pieces of wood as necessary. Be careful not to add too much fuel to the fire because you don't want it to get out of control.

Sitting around a campfire at the end of a long day is a great way to wrap the day up. It's easy to get comfortable around the fire, but you do need to keep a few responsibilities in mind while maintaining and enjoying your fire. Children and pets should be supervised and kept under control while around the fire. Kids and pets are naturally curious about fire and should never be left unattended when there's a fire burning. Unattended children have been known to throw all sorts of items in campfires, from aerosol cans that explode when heated to aluminum cans, which break down into dangerous aluminum dust in a campfire. We once went camping with a family who had a young child throw her Gameboy into the fire. Luckily they noticed what she'd done before she reached in to grab it.

In addition to keeping an eye on your kids and pets, it's your responsibility to keep an eye on your fire as well. A burning or smoldering fire should never be left unattended. When you're done for the night and ready to go to bed, put your campfire out. If it's hot to the touch, it's still dangerous and shouldn't be left unattended.

The easiest way to put out a campfire is with water, and it's going to take lots of it. Pour water on the campfire until it stops hissing and steaming and then stir the wet ashes and embers until you're sure everything is out.

Dirt can be added to the fire to put it out if you're trying to conserve water. Add a few shovelfuls of dirt and stir it in. Then add more and stir again. Burying a fire won't put it out. You have to continuously add dirt and stir until the fire is extinguished.

Campfire Fun

Looking for some fun and safe ways to entertain the family around the campfire? Here are some of the ways people have fun while sitting around a fire:

- Campfire songs. You can sing popular songs like Kumbayah and Michael Finnigan or you can bring a radio and listen to and sing family favorites.
- Chubby bunny. The goal of this game is to be the person who can place the most jumbo marshmallows in their mouth at once and still be able to say "Chubby Bunny." Yes, it's immature and childish. It's also fun and sure to get the whole family laughing.
- Roast marshmallows. Get a stick or a metal fork designed for roasting marshmallows and impale a marshmallow on the end of it. Put it close to the fire and toast it until it's golden brown. Children must be supervised while roasting marshmallows because they can catch on fire and hot marshmallow can drip and burn kids that aren't careful.
- Roasted strawberries. Here's one most people have never heard of. Dip a strawberry in marshmallow fluff and roast it over the campfire. These are delicious and are a good way to ensure your kids eat their fruit while camping.
- Orange rind chocolate cakes. Cut the top ¼ off of a large orange and scoop out the meat. You'll be left with a hollow rounded shell. Whip up a box or two of cupcake mix. Fill the orange rind ¾ of the way with batter. Place the top back on the orange, wrap it in foil and place it in the fire. Let it cook for 15 to 20 minutes, or until the batter is cooked all the way through. Let cool for 5 minutes and serve topped with frosting or whipped cream.
- Make s'mores. This is a favorite of families across North America. You're going to need graham crackers, large marshmallows and milk chocolate bars. Break the graham cracker in half and place a piece of chocolate on one half. Roast a marshmallow and sandwich it between the graham

cracker halves. Let it sit for 30 seconds to a minute so the chocolate will start to melt and enjoy.
- Tell ghost stories. Older kids will love this one. With little kids your mileage may vary. My son loves ghost stories, but a 6-year old friend of his we brought along one time hated them.

Camping Recipes

This section contains recipes you can whip up while camping. I've tried to keep them as easy as possible because most people don't want to whip up a gourmet meal while standing in a campsite. These recipes are mainly comfort foods that are filling and will replenish calories lost during a busy day, so you won't be exhausted while out and about.

Bacon, Egg, Sausage and Potato Omelet

Ingredients:
2 cups bacon, cooked and crumbled
2 cups sausage, cooked and crumbled
3 medium potatoes
½ onion
7 eggs
Salt
Pepper

Directions:
1. Fry the bacon and cook the sausage and crumble each up into chunks.
2. Slice the potatoes. Leave the peels on.
3. Dice the onion and add it to the bacon and sausage.
4. Add the potatoes to the bacon and sausage.
5. Partially scramble the eggs in a separate skillet.
6. Add the meat and the potatoes to the eggs and finish cooking.

Balsamic Barbecued Steak

Ingredients:
2 pounds Sirloin steak
1 cup balsamic vinegar
¼ cup olive oil

4 tablespoons honey
2 tablespoons garlic powder
Salt and pepper, to taste

Directions:
1. Add all ingredients except steak to a bowl and whisk together.
2. Place steak and sauce in a resealable plastic bag and shake until the steak is coated.
3. Let steak marinate for at least 6 hours.
4. Barbecue on barbecue grill or on grill placed over campfire.

BBQ Beef Ribs

Ingredients:
Ribs
Beef Glaze Ingredients:
1 cup honey
½ cup apple juice
¼ cup brown sugar
4 tablespoons Dijon mustard
Beef Rub Ingredients:
1 teaspoon salt
1 teaspoon cayenne pepper
1 teaspoon black pepper
Directions:
1. Lightly coat ribs with vegetable oil.
2. Combine salt and peppers and rub into the ribs before cooking.
3. Prepare barbecue and move hot coals to one side of the barbecue. You're going to use indirect heat to barbecue the ribs.
4. Sear the ribs by cooking them over direct heat for 2 minutes on each side.
5. Place a drip pan under the ribs and place them on the opposite side of the grill as the coals.
6. Cook ribs for 2 hours. Add new coals to the barbecue as needed.
7. Flip the ribs over and cook for another 1 to 2 hours, or until meat is ready to fall off the bone.
8. Combine glaze ingredients.
9. Brush glaze onto ribs. Use generous amounts of glaze.
10. Cook for another 15 minutes.
11. Serve hot.

BBQ Chicken

Ingredients:
Chicken legs and thighs

Rub Ingredients:
¼ cup sea salt
¼ cup granulated sugar
3 tablespoons ground cumin
3 tablespoons paprika
1 tablespoon mustard powder
1 tablespoon chili powder
1 tablespoon cayenne pepper
1 tablespoon garlic powder

Sauce Ingredients:
¼ cup water
½ cup Worcestershire sauce
¼ cup brown sugar
1 tablespoon honey
1 tablespoon agave nectar
2 tablespoons yellow mustard
1 teaspoon soy sauce
1 tablespoon liquid smoke

Directions:
1. Add the rub ingredients to a large freezer bag and shake up until blended.
2. Place chicken in the freezer bag and shake until coated with rub.
3. Return the chicken to the ice chest and let it sit on ice for at least 3 hours. Alternatively, you can prepare the chicken and rub before you leave on your trip and put it on ice until you're ready to cook it.
4. Add all of the sauce ingredients to a saucepan and let simmer for 15 to 20 minutes, or until sauce starts to thicken.
5. Prepare barbecue by starting coals and moving them all to one side of the grill.
6. Remove chicken from bag and place on the opposite side of the grill.
7. Cook over indirect heat for 25 to 35 minutes, or until chicken starts to brown on both sides.

8. Slather BBQ sauce over the chicken pieces and place the pieces directly over the coals.
9. Cook until chicken is cooked all the way through and skin is nice and crispy. Be sure to flip the chicken regularly.

Beans and Franks

Ingredients:
6 to 10 hot dogs
5 slices bacon
2 cans kidney beans
Sauce Ingredients:
2 cans tomato sauce
½ cup ketchup
½ cup flour
1 tablespoon brown sugar
2 tablespoons Worcestershire sauce
1 teaspoon salt
Directions:
1. Cook bacon in skillet and break into pieces.
2. Add all of the sauce ingredients to a pot and stir together over medium heat.
3. Bring to a simmer and stir until the sauce starts to thicken.
4. Add the bacon and kidney beans.
5. Cut the hot dogs into coins and add them to the pot.
6. Cook until hot dogs are warmed all the way through.

Breakfast Burritos

Ingredients:
10 sausages
5 eggs
2 potatoes, peeled and cubed
1 cup cheddar cheese, shredded
Salsa
Tortillas

Non-stick cooking spray

Directions:
1. Cook sausage in a skillet.
2. Remove sausage from skillet and crumble it up or break it into chunks.
3. Slice the potatoes.
4. Spray non-stick cooking spray in skillet and brown potatoes.
5. Add sausage back into skillet, along with the eggs.
6. Cook until eggs are done.
7. Warm tortillas and fill up with the sausage, eggs and potatoes.
8. Sprinkle cheese on top.
9. Add salsa, to taste.
10. Serve warm.

Campfire Baked Potato

Ingredients:
Potatoes
Aluminum foil
Desired toppings

Directions:
1. Wash potatoes and poke holes in them with a fork.
2. Wrap each potato individually in aluminum foil.
3. Double-wrap each potato with another layer of aluminum foil.
4. Place potatoes directly on the hot coals in the campfire.
5. Bake for 30 to 45 minutes, or until potatoes are soft.
6. Let cool for 10 minutes.
7. Remove potatoes from foil.
8. Season with desired toppings and serve warm.

Clam Chowder

NOTE: This recipe can be cooked in a pot over a camp stove burner or on a heavy grill placed over the campfire. It can also be prepared in a Dutch oven, which is my favorite way to cook it.

Ingredients:
2 cans of chopped clams
2 cups half-n-half
1 cup of clam juice
1 cup water
5 thick cut slices of bacon
2 sticks of celery, chopped
1 large onion, chopped
4 potatoes, peeled and cubed
2 garlic cloves, minced
½ cup flour
1 chicken bouillon cube
½ teaspoon sea salt
½ teaspoon black pepper
½ teaspoon cayenne pepper (optional)

Bread bowls, optional

Directions:
1. Add bacon and a teaspoon of oil to the pot or Dutch oven and cook until crispy.
2. Break bacon into pieces.
3. Add onions, garlic and celery to pot and cook in bacon drippings.
4. Combine flour, water and half-n-half in a bowl and stir until smooth.
5. Add all ingredients except clams to pot or Dutch oven and bring to a rolling boil for 20 to 30 minutes, or until potatoes are soft.
6. Add clams a couple minutes before the chowder is complete. Add them too soon and the clams will get tough.
7. Serve hot. This clam chowder is absolutely delicious when served in a sourdough bread bowl.

Dutch Oven Baked Beans

NOTE: This recipe requires that you prepare the beans at home and simply reheat them when you get to the campsite. Alternatively, you can add all of the ingredients to a Dutch oven and cook them by placing the Dutch oven in the campfire, covering it with coals and letting it cook for 4 to 6 hours, or until the beans are soft.

Ingredients:
2 cups bacon, cooked and crumbled
4 cups white beans
2 onions, chopped
15 cups water
2 cups brown sugar, packed
½ cup BBQ sauce
½ cup molasses
3 teaspoons mustard
1 teaspoon garlic powder
2 teaspoons salt
1 teaspoon pepper

Directions:
1. Bring water to a boil in a large saucepan.
2. Boil beans for a few minutes until they start to soften up.
3. Add all ingredients to a Dutch oven and stir.
4. Preheat oven to 350 degrees F.
5. Place Dutch oven on bottom rack in oven and bake for 6 hours, stirring occasionally. Add water halfway through if the beans thicken up too much.
6. Store beans in a freezer bag and reheat when you want to eat them at the campsite. They go well with barbecued foods. Alternatively, you can cut hot dogs up or add smokies to them for delicious beanie weenies your kids will love.

Dutch Oven Cinnamon Caramel Monkey Bread

Ingredients:
3 canisters of Pillsbury biscuits

4 teaspoons cinnamon
1 cup brown sugar, packed
1 cup granulated sugar
1 stick butter
½ cup caramel

Directions:
1. Mix cinnamon, sugar and brown sugar together.
2. Tear biscuits into chunks and roll around in the cinnamon sugar mixture. Make sure each piece is well-coated.
3. Place the biscuit pieces in a Dutch oven.
4. Melt the butter and pour it over the top of the biscuit pieces.
5. Place lid on Dutch oven and place it in the coals of the campfire. Place hot coals on top of Dutch oven.
6. Cook for 35 to 45 minutes, or until monkey bread is cooked all the way through.
7. Remove Dutch oven from fire and let cool for 15 minutes.
8. Remove lid and drizzle caramel over the monkey bread.
9. Serve warm.

Dutch Oven Chili Macaroni

Ingredients:
2 pounds hamburger
3 cups macaroni
2 onions, chopped
3 cups diced tomatoes
1 cup tomato sauce
½ cup chilies, diced
1 teaspoon cayenne pepper
1 tablespoon chili powder
1 tablespoon dried minced onion
2 teaspoons salt
1 cup Mexican blend cheese, for topping

Directions:
1. Place Dutch oven over hot coals in campfire.
2. Let the Dutch oven heat up for 10 minutes.
3. Add hamburger and onion to Dutch oven and cook until hamburger is browned and the onions start to soften.
4. Add the rest of the ingredients and stir together.
5. Place lid on Dutch oven and cover with hot coals.
6. Let cook for 30 to 60 minutes, or until macaroni is soft.
7. Remove Dutch oven from fire.
8. Sprinkle cheese on chili macaroni as it is served.

Dutch Oven Fruit Pie

NOTE: This recipe calls for berry pie filling, but you can use cans of whatever filling you'd like. You can also make your own filling by cutting fruit and combining it with sugar and a bit of water and cooking it until it gets soft.

Ingredients:
1 can berry pie filling
1 box muffin mix
2 tablespoons butter
1 aluminum pie tin
Whipped cream, for topping

Directions:
1. Open berry pie filling can and pour contents into the pie tin.
2. Pour box of muffin mix over the top of the filling.
3. Distribute small pieces of butter over the top of the muffin mix.
4. Place the Dutch oven in the coals.
5. Set the pie tin in the Dutch oven. In order to ensure the pie cooks evenly, place a few stones in the bottom of the Dutch oven and set the pie tin on top of the stones.
6. Put the lid on the Dutch oven and cover the Dutch oven with hot coals.
7. Let cook for 15 to 20 minutes.
8. Remove pie from Dutch oven and let cool for 5 to 10 minutes.
9. Spoon fruit pie onto a plate and add whipped cream on top.
10. Serve warm.

Eggs in a Nest

Ingredients:
Eggs
Butter
Bread
Salt
Pepper

Directions:
1. Cut a hole out from the center of a slice of bread. You can use the rim of a small glass to make a clean cut.
2. Heat a skillet over medium heat.
3. Add a generous amount of butter to the skillet and let it melt.
4. Place the bread in the skillet.
5. Crack an egg and dump the contents into the hole you created in step 1.
6. Salt and pepper the egg, to taste.
7. Let the egg cook for 2 minutes and then flip the slice of bread over, keeping the egg in the hole.
8. Add a bit more salt and pepper, if so desired.
9. Let the egg cook until it reaches the desired consistency. You can cook it so the egg yolk is runny or you can leave it in long enough so the yolk gets hard.

Fire-Roasted Cinnamon Apple

Ingredients:
1 apple
½ cup sugar
1 tablespoon cinnamon
1 skewer

Directions:
1. Mix sugar and cinnamon together in a mixing bowl.
2. Push skewer into the apple.
3. Roast the apple over the open flame of a campfire.

4. Carefully peel the apple. It will be extremely hot when it first comes out of the fire, so be careful. Young children should be helped by adults.
5. Roll the apple around in the cinnamon-sugar mixture.
6. Let the apple cool a bit and eat it warm.

Five Alarm Dutch Oven Chili

WARNING: This chili has quite a kick to it and isn't for the faint of heart. It can also cause a bit of gastric distress, which is the reason why my husband has been banned from making it while we're camping. It is good, though, if spicy chili is your thing.

Ingredients:
2 pounds ground beef
3 cans pinto beans
3 cups canned diced tomatoes, with chilies
¼ cup water
½ cup tomato paste
1 large onion, diced
2 cloves garlic, minced
3 habanero peppers, seeded and diced
3 jalapeno peppers, seeded and diced
1 table spoon olive oil
3 tablespoons chili powder
2 teaspoons ground cumin
2 teaspoons oregano
2 teaspoons cayenne pepper

Directions:
1. Place Dutch oven on hot coals in the campfire.
2. Let it heat up until hot enough to brown ground beef.
3. Add 1 tablespoon of olive oil to the bottom of the oven and spread it around.
4. Add the ground beef to the oven and cook until it starts to brown.
5. Add onions and garlic and cook until onions start to turn clear.
6. Add the rest of the ingredients, except for the beans.
7. Place lid on Dutch oven and let cook for 45 minutes.
8. Remove lid and add pinto beans. Stir them in.
9. Let cook for an additional hour with the lid off.
10. Serve chili hot.

Killer Kabobs

Ingredients:
1 pound beef, cubed
1 pound chicken, cubed
1 pound shrimp, peeled and deveined
4 large bell peppers, cut into squares
4 large onions, cut into pieces
1 pound small mushrooms

Sauce Ingredients:
6 tablespoons soy sauce
6 tablespoons extra virgin olive oil
1 tablespoon garlic powder
1 teaspoon lime juice

Directions:
1. This recipe works best when the kabob ingredients are allowed to marinate in the sauce.
2. Combine sauce ingredients in a large bag and shake until blended.
3. Cut meat and veggies and place them in separate bags with the sauce.
4. Let marinate for at least 6 hours. I like to make my kabobs at home before I leave and leave them marinating in the cooler for at least a day.
5. Remove contents from bag and place them on skewers, alternating meat and vegetables. Continue until all of the meat and veggies have been placed on skewers.
6. This recipe will make 8 to 12 kabobs, depending on how much you fill them.

Quick and Easy Pancakes

NOTE: These pancakes can be cooked on a skillet or a flat metal surface placed over a barbecue grill. They can also be cooked on the inside of a Dutch oven lid. Flip the lid over and place the top of the lid in the coals. Cook the pancakes on the flat undersurface of the lid.

Ingredients:
1 cup flour
1 egg
1 cup milk
1 tablespoon melted butter
1 ½ teaspoons baking powder
¼ teaspoon salt
Vegetable oil, for cooking surface

Directions:
1. Combine all ingredients except flour and melted butter in a bowl and whisk together.
2. Add the flour slowly and stir until smooth.
3. Melt butter and stir it in.
4. Heat up cooking surface and add a small amount of vegetable oil.
5. Pour ½ cup of batter on the cooking surface.
6. Cook until the top starts to bubble and the edges start to brown.
7. Flip pancake and cook until the other side is brown.
8. Serve with your favorite toppings. Maple syrup and whipped cream are both tasty, as are many jams and jellies.

Traditional Banana Boat

Ingredients:
1 banana
5 to 10 marshmallows
1 bar of milk chocolate

Directions:
1. Peel banana.
2. Cut it in half lengthwise.
3. Place the bottom half of the banana boat on a piece of aluminum foil.
4. Use a spoon to dig a groove into the banana slice on the bottom, so it'll hold the chocolate and marshmallows.
5. Break chocolate bar into chunks.

6. Sprinkle marshmallows and chocolate chunks on the bottom half of the banana.
7. Place the top half of the banana over the bottom half and wrap in foil so the chocolate and marshmallows are held in place.
8. Place on hot coals in campfire for 10 to 15 minutes, or until the chocolate and marshmallows are melted.
9. Let cool for 5 minutes.
10. Unwrap and eat while warm and gooey.

Bonus Chapter: Campfire Desserts

This bonus chapter is packed full of delicious and easy to make desserts the whole family will love. I've included perennial favorites like s'mores and banana boats, along with a few surprises you probably haven't heard of.

These recipes are fun to make and are a great way to keep the kids in your group entertained. Be sure to supervise children every step of the way, as these recipes can be extremely hot and can cause severe burns if caution isn't exercise. The foil-wrapped desserts will often emit extremely hot steam when first opened, so this step is best done by an adult.

What are you waiting for? It's time for dessert!

Banana Boats

Serving size:
1 serving
Cooking method:
Foil-wrapping
Ingredients:
1 banana
Chocolate chips
Marshmallows
Directions:
1. Peel the banana and cut it in half lengthwise.
2. Place half of the banana on a piece of foil.
3. Add chocolate chips and marshmallows to the piece of banana and place the other half of the banana on top.
4. Wrap in foil to hold it all in place.
5. Alternatively, you can cut a slit into a whole banana, open it up and fill the opening with chocolate chips and marshmallows and then wrap the banana peel and all in foil.
6. Place the banana boat directly into the embers of the fire.

7. Cook for 10 to 15 minutes, or until the marshmallows and chocolate have melted.
8. Let cool for a few minutes, unwrap and serve.

Chocolate Banana Burritos

Serving size:
1 serving
Cooking method:
Foil-wrapping
Ingredients:
1 banana
1 flour tortilla
1 tablespoon peanut butter
1 tablespoon chopped almonds
Chocolate chips
Marshmallows
Directions:
1. Lay tortilla flat and spread peanut butter on it.
2. Cut banana up and spread it out on tortilla.
3. Add almonds, chocolate chips and marshmallows.
4. Fold tortilla like you would a regular burrito.
5. Wrap in foil.
6. Place foil wrap in campfire for 10 minutes, or until ingredients are completely melted.
7. Be careful when opening the foil packet because contents can be extremely hot.
8. Let cool until lukewarm and serve.

Cinnamon-Sugar Apple Sauce

Serving size:
1 serving
Cooking method:
Foil-wrapping
Ingredients:
1 apple
1 tablespoon cinnamon
1 tablespoon sugar
Directions:

1. Core the apple. When you're done there should be a hole straight through the center of the apple.
2. Wrap foil partially around the apple to cover one of the holes.
3. Combine the cinnamon and sugar and place it in the exposed hole.
4. Finish wrapping the apple in foil.
5. Place in hot coals of campfire.
6. Cook for 10 to 15 minutes, or until soft.
7. Remove from fire and let cool for 10 minutes.
8. Mash apple up with fork until it's the consistency of applesauce. You can leave the skin or you can remove it.

Coconut Bread

Serving size:
1 serving
Cooking method:
Skewer
Ingredients:
1 piece of French bread
½ cup whole milk
¼ cup sugar
¼ cup shredded coconut
Directions:
1. Skewer bread so the skewer goes through the hard crust.
2. Warm milk in saucepan and stir sugar into it.
3. Dip bread into sugar milk.
4. Roll it around in shredded coconut.
5. Cook it over the campfire until golden brown.
6. Let cool until lukewarm and enjoy.

Ice Chest Fudge

Serving size:
4 to 6 servings
Cooking method:
None
Ingredients:
2 cups powdered sugar
½ cup cream cheese
½ cup cocoa powder
2 tablespoons butter
Chopped almonds, walnuts or pecans (optional)
Directions:
1. Add all of the ingredients to a large freezer bag.
2. Seal the bag and mix the contents by squishing and squeezing the bag.
3. Once the contents are thoroughly mixed, place the bag in an ice chest for 15 to 20 minutes to thicken the fudge.

Orange Brownies

Serving size:
6 servings

Cooking method:
Foil-wrapping

Ingredients:
6 oranges
Box of brownie mix
Container of chocolate frosting

Directions:
1. Cut the top 1/3 off of the oranges.
2. Scoop out the meat of the orange, so you have a hollow shell.
3. Whip up the brownie mix per the directions on the box.
4. Fill each orange 2/3 of the way full with brownie mix.
5. Place the top on the orange and wrap it in foil, so the top is held in place.
6. Place the foil-wrapped orange in the embers of the fire and bake for 10 to 20 minutes, or until brownie is cooked all the way through.
7. Let cool.
8. Frost and enjoy.

Orange Cupcakes

Serving size:
6 servings
Cooking method:
Foil-wrapping
Ingredients:
6 oranges
Box of cupcake mix
Container of cream cheese frosting
Directions:
1. Cut the top 1/3 off of the oranges.
2. Scoop out the meat of the orange, so you have a hollow shell.
3. Whip up the cupcake mix per the directions on the box.
4. Fill each orange 2/3 of the way full with cupcake mix.
5. Place the top on the orange and wrap it in foil, so the top is held in place.
6. Place the foil-wrapped orange in the embers of the fire and bake for 10 to 20 minutes, or until cupcake is cooked all the way through.
7. Let cool.
8. Frost and enjoy.

Oreo Pudding Pie

Serving size:
6 to 8 servings
Cooking method:
None
Ingredients:
1 graham cracker pie crust
4 cups milk
A can of whipped cream
1 package Oreo cookies
1 box instant vanilla pudding
1 box instant chocolate pudding

Directions:
1. Make the vanilla pudding by adding two cup of milk to the mix and whisking it for 3 minutes. Let it sit for 5 minutes to set.
2. Do the same with the chocolate pudding. You can make it while you're waiting for the vanilla pudding to set.
3. Fill the bottom half of the graham cracker crust with vanilla pudding.
4. Fill it the rest of the way with chocolate pudding.
5. Cover the top of the pie with whipped cream.
6. Crumble Oreo cookies over the top.
7. Cover with aluminum foil and let chill in an ice chest until serving time.

Personal Fruit Pies

Serving size:
4 to 6 servings
Cooking method:
Skillet on a grill
Ingredients:
1 can of instant biscuit mix
1 can of pie filling
Directions:
1. Roll each biscuit out until it's flat.
2. Place 3 teaspoons of your favorite pie filling in the center of the biscuit.
3. Fold the edges up to cover the filling.
4. Cook in a skillet over the campfire or the barbecue grill. The pies are done when they're a golden brown color.
5. Top with whipped cream or powdered sugar and enjoy.

Pineapple Donut Delight

Serving size:
1 serving
Cooking method:
Foil-wrapping
Ingredients:
1 unfrosted cake donut
½ cup pineapple chunks
1 tablespoon butter
2 tablespoons brown sugar
½ teaspoon cinnamon
Directions:
1. Break donut into pieces and place on piece of foil.
2. Melt butter and add brown sugar and cinnamon to it. Spread it out across the top of the donut.
3. Add pineapple chunks to the top.
4. Wrap in foil.

5. Cook for 8 to 12 minutes by placing foil packet directly in hot coals.
6. Let cool for 10 minutes and serve warm.

Rocky Road Cones

Serving size:
1 serving
Cooking method:
Foil-wrapping
Ingredients:
1 sugar cone
A handful of marshmallows
Chocolate chips
1 tablespoon of chunky peanut butter
Directions:
1. Add peanut butter to the inside of the cone.
2. Fill with marshmallows and chocolate chips.
3. Wrap the cone in aluminum foil.
4. Place foil wrap in campfire for 5 minutes.
5. Flip over and leave in campfire an additional 5 minutes.
6. Remove from campfire and let cool for 5 minutes.
7. Unwrap and enjoy. Be careful because the marshmallow and chocolate can get really hot.

S'Mores

Serving size:
1 serving
Cooking method:
Skewer
Ingredients:
Graham crackers
Jumbo marshmallows
Milk chocolate bars
Directions:
1. Place a jumbo marshmallow on a skewer and cook it over the campfire until golden brown.

2. Place a piece of chocolate and the toasted marshmallow on a piece of graham cracker and create a sandwich by placing another piece of graham cracker over the top.
3. Wait 60 seconds, so the chocolate starts to melt and the marshmallow cools a bit and enjoy.

Strawberry S'Mores

Serving size:
1 serving
Cooking method:
Skewer
Ingredients:
Graham crackers
Jumbo marshmallows
Milk chocolate bars
Sliced strawberries
Directions:
1. Place a jumbo marshmallow on a skewer and cook it over the campfire until golden brown.
2. Place a piece of chocolate, a few pieces of strawberry and the toasted marshmallow on a piece of graham cracker and create a sandwich by placing another piece of graham cracker over the top.
3. Wait 60 seconds, so the chocolate starts to melt and the marshmallow cools a bit and enjoy.

Part 2

Main Dishes

30 Minute Goulash

Ingredients
- 3 Tbsp oil and/or butter
- 2 cloves garlic (or 1/2 teaspoon powdered garlic)
- 1 large onion
- 1 pound(s) ground beef
- 1 26 ounce can of whole tomatoes
- 1/2 tsp dill seed
- 1 tsp parsley
- salt and pepper to taste

Directions
1. In 3 tbsp of oil or butter, saute 2 cloves of fresh garlic, peeled and chopped (or later, when browning the meat, add 1/2 to 1 tsp of powdered garlic, depending on your taste. While the garlic is simmering, peel and slice (about 1/4' thick slices) 1 large onion (of any kind). Do not chop. Add it in its whole rings, and turn up the heat all the way. When the onions are soft and beginning to brown, add 1 lb of ground beef, not too lean as fat adds flavor. Mix with the onion and garlic and cook until brown (at this point, if you are really concerned with fat and chlorestorol, drain exceess fat). Add salt and pepper to taste. While the meat is browning, open a 26 oz can of whole tomatoes. When the meat is brown, add the juice from the can and the tomatoes, tearing them into small pieces with your fingers. This creates a juice, rather than a gravy. If the tomatoes come in a thick sauce, add water until it becomes juicelike. This is important, since it will be served over rice. Add 1/2 tsp of dill seed and 1 tsp of dried (or fresh,

chopped) parsley. Cover and simmer. Cook 1 cup or your favorite rice. When the rice is done, so is the goulash. Place 1/2 cup of rice on each plate and cover with goulash, making sure to serve with plenty of juice. A salad and brown-and-serve dinner rolls go well with this, too.

A Mean Three-Bean Salad

Ingredients
- 2 15 oz. cans pinto beans
- 2 15 oz. cans kidney beans
- 2 15 oz. cans garbanzo beans
- 1 c red onion, thinly sliced
- 1 c green bell pepper, chopped
- 1 c red bell pepper, chopped
- 1/2 c celery
- 3/4 c red wine vinegar
- 1/2 c sugar
- 1/2 c olive oil
- 1/2 tsp dry mustard
- 1/2 tsp salt
- 2 Tbsp parsley, chopped
- 1 Tbsp fresh cilantro, chopped
- 1 tsp fresh oregano, chopped

Directions
1. Drain all the beans; put into a large mixing bowl. Add red onion, bell peppers and celery. In small bowl, combine vinegar, sugar, olive oil, salt, mustard, cilantro, parsley, and oregano. Pour over beans and veggies; toss to mix well. Cover and refrigerate several hours or overnight, stirring occasionally.

Ain't Plain Mashed Potatoes

Makes: **12**

Ingredients
- 8 c mashed potatoes
- 4 strips bacon, diced
- 2 medium onions, thinly sliced
- 1 c Parmesan cheese, freshly grated
- 3 cloves garlic, minced
- 2 Tbsp fresh parsley, chopped
- 1 stick butter
- salt and pepper to taste

Directions
1. Peel and boil potatoes; drain. Fry bacon until crisp; add onion and cook for five minutes, adding garlic near the end. Add bacon mixture and butter to potatoes, mixing thoroughly. Add seasonings as desired.

All Fruit Salad

Ingredients
- watermelon
- cantelope
- green or red grapes
- apples
- pineapple
- strawberries
- blueberries
- raspberries
- oranges
- grapefruit

Directions
1. Mix all fruit together - sweeten with sugar if you want and then top fruit with bananas around the edge and in the

center. Serve in bowls, and top with whipped creme and a cherry.

All in One Burger and Sides

Ingredients
- Hamburger
- Potatoes
- Corn on the Cob

Directions
1. Make a hamburger patty with your seasoning. My grandkids like onion flakes and seasoning salt. We prefer onions slices to our patty. Cut a potato slice about 2" thick. Then we put a corn on the cob, one that is about 4" long. We then wrap all this in aluminum foil and seal. We cook this on the grill about 30 minutes to 45 minutes. You have a complete meal in one wrap.
2. We also do the same think with sausage and hash browns in the morning.

Amarillo Steak

Ingredients
- 2 - 2.5 pound(s) lean beef: Top Round, Flank steak or London Broil
- 1/3 c virgin olive oil
- 1/3 c reconstituted lemon juice or juice of one lemon
- 2 cloves garlic, crushed or equivalent dried
- 1/4 tsp salt
- 1/4 tsp pepper

Directions
1. Combine marinade ingredients in a ziplock freezer bag and add steak. Refrigerate 6-8 hours. Remove steak and discard marinade. Grill steak over medium heat about 10 minutes per side or to desired doneness. For medium doneness that's

about 150 degrees. Transfer steak to cutting board and allow to sit for 10 minutes. Slice diagonally across the grain into thin strips.
2. Great with a cold potato salad on a summer day! Refrigerated leftover strips are wonderful on a sandwich or salad the next day.

Antipasta Dip

Ingredients
- 2 large tomatoes (finely chopped)
- 1 small can chopped green chilis
- 1 small can chopped black olives
- 3 Tbsp olive oil
- 3 or 4 green onions (chopped)
- 1 1/2 Tbsp vinegar
- 1 green pepper (finely chopped)
- 1 small jar chopped pimento
- 1 Tbsp garlic salt

Directions
1. Mix all ingredients together and marinate in refrigerator for a while. Serve as dip with nacho chips

Arkansas Potatoes

Ingredients
- 1 package fully cooked smoked sausage, sliced
- 1 large onion
- several small red/yellow potatoes
- salt and pepper
- seasoning salt

Directions

1. Slice onion and potatoes and place in fire proof skillet. Add water to keep from scorching. Add seasonings to taste along with smoked sausage. Cook for 20 minutes.

Asian Marinade

Makes: **2**

Ingredients
- 1/4 c soy sauce
- 3 Tbsp honey
- 2 Tbsp vinegar
- 3/4 c olive oil
- 2 green onions, finely chopped
- 1 1/2 tsp garlic powder
- 1 1/2 tsp ground ginger

Directions
1. Wisk together all ingredients in a medium sized bowl, and pour into a zip lock bag or airtight container. This recipe marinates up to 2 pounds of meat.

Aunt Karnie's Pasta Salad

Ingredients
- 4 boneless, skinless chicken breast
- 1 bottle of Italian salad dressing
- 1 Tbsp Rose's Lime Juice
- 1/4 c honey
- 1 bag cooked fusili pasta
- 1 c chopped red onion
- 2 c Caesar dressing
- 4 Roma tomatoes, seeded and chopped

Directions
1. Marinate chicken breasts in the Italian Dressing, lime juice & honey for about 3+ hours. Fry chicken in a cast iron skillet for about 5 minutes on each side. Add the rest of the marinade. Bring to a boil then simmer for about 30 minutes. Cut the chicken into cubes and add to cooked pasta, red onion, Caesar dressing & tomatoes. Chill & serve.

"Auntie Jillaine's" Newyork/Maryland Crab Cakes

Ingredients
- 1 pound(s) fresh lump crab meat
- 1 c low-fat mayonnaise
- 1 Tbsp Dijon or dry mustard
- 1 egg, beaten
- 1 tsp Worcestershire sauce
- 1 tsp dry white wine
- 1 tsp Old Bay seasoning
- juice of lemon
- 7 saltine crackers, crushed
- 2 Tbsp fresh minced parsley
- 1/4 tsp garlic powder

Directions
1. Put crab meat in bowl. Mix rest of ingredients and add to crab meat. Chill for 2 hours. Form into 6 to 8 cakes. Place on buttered sheet pan and bake at 450 degrees until golden brown.

Awesome Chip or Vegetable Dip

Ingredients

- 1 package Ranch dressing mix
- 1 container cottage cheese
- 1 container sour cream

Directions
1. Mix together and put in fridge - the longer it sits, the stronger it gets!

Baby Red Potatoes

Makes: **6**

Ingredients
- Approximately 20 baby red potatoes
- 1 packet dry Italian dressing mix
- Olive oil

Directions
1. Cut potatoes into bite-sized pieces. Place in a large bowl, toss with Olive oil until lightly coated. Sprinkle dressing mix over potatoes and toss until all sides are covered. Wrap in foil, put near coals or on BBQ grill until potatoes are fork tender. Potatoes can also be cooked spread in a baking sheet and put in over for 45 minutes at 350 degrees.

Backwoods Chili Rice Skillet

Makes: **8**

Ingredients
- 1 pound(s) ground beef
- 4 c Uncle Ben's Quick brand rice
- 3 c water
- 1 c chopped onion
- 1 large green pepper, chopped
- 1 package chili seasoning mix

- 1 can tomatoes, undrained
- 1 can kidney beans, drained
- 1 Tbsp salt
- 1 c shredded Cheddar or Monterey Jack cheese

Directions
1. In a large skillet, brown meat, drain. Add remaining ingredients except cheese; stir. Bring to a vigorous boil. Cover tightly. Simmer about 5 minutes or until desired consistency. Sprinkle with cheese.

Bacon & Cheddar Grilled Cheese Sandwich

Makes: **1**

Ingredients
- bread (we like raisin bread)
- bacon (we use leftover bacon from breakfast)
- cheddar cheese
- olive oil spray

Directions
1. Place bacon and cheese between slices of bread. Spray cooking surface with oilive oil and toast on a skillet over an RV stove or in a Coleman sandwich toaster over the fire.

Bacon Tortilla Rolls

Ingredients
- 1 c mayonnaise
- 1 c sour cream
- bacon or 1/2 jar Bacos
- 2 packages frozen chopped spinach (cooked and drained)
- 1/2 package Ranch House dry dressing (buttermilk)
- flour tortillas

Directions
1. Mix all of the above (except tortillas) at least 2 hours in advance. Roll the mixture in tortillas. Put in refrigerator at least 2 hours before slicing. Slice about ¼" thick.

Baked Beans

Ingredients
- 1 Large can of Bush's original baked beans - Industrial size
- 1 pound(s) Bacon cooked and broken into pieces and all the grease too!
- 1 White onion - chopped
- 1 c Pure maple syrup

Directions
1. Add all ingredients together (including all the bacon grease) in a slow cooker and cook on low for 8 hours - Enjoy!

Baked Lima Beans

Ingredients
- 1 large can Butter Beans, drained
- 1 can tomato soup
- 2 onions, grated
- 1 c brown sugar

Directions
1. Mix all ingredients and bake 1 hour at 375 degrees.

Baked Onions

Ingredients
- onion per person

- black pepper
- butter or margarine

Directions
1. Take an onion and take off outer skin. Hollow out the core and add cracked fresh ground black pepper and put a large pat of butter or margarine in the hole. Wrap in aluminum foil and bake on grill for about an hour on medium, or in oven at 325 degrees for an hour. The onion is juicy, sweet and delicious.

Baked Potato in a Can

Ingredients
- 1 medium size potato
- butter
- salt
- pepper
- heavy duty aluminum foil
- tin can (from veggies or beans)

Directions
1. Clean the potato. Butter the outside of the potato really well, and season to taste. Put potato into the tin can and cover top of can with foil. Place the tin can next to a fire pit of coals and let it set for 25 minutes, then turn can 90° and cook for another 20 minutes (do not peek at potato). After 45 minutes you will have a perfect baked potato.

Baked Santa Fe Dip

Ingredients
- 2 c shredded cheddar cheese
- 1/2 c light mayonnaise

- 1 c shredded Monterrey Jack cheese
- 1/4 tsp garlic powder
- 1 8 ounce can whole kernel corn (drained)
- 1 medium tomato (seeded & chopped)
- 1 4 ounce can chopped green chili peppers
- 1/4 c sliced green onion
- 2 tsp canned chipotle chili peppers in adobe sauce (finely chopped)
- 2 Tbsp fresh cilantro (snipped)

Directions
1. Stir together cheeses, mayo, corn, chili peppers, chipotle chili peppers & garlic powder. Spread mixture into a shallow one quart casserole. Cover and chill up to 24 hours. Combine tomato, green onions and cilantro. Cover and chill up to 24 hours. When ready to serve, bake cheese mixture in 350 degree oven for 25 minutes, until bubbly. Spoon tomato mixture on top in center and serve with tortilla chips.

Balsamic Steak

Ingredients
- 1 pound(s) top sirloin steak
- 1/2 c balsamic vinegar
- 1/4 c olive oil
- 1-2 tsp minced garlic
- 2 Tbsp honey or brown sugar
- dash Worcestershire sauce
- salt and pepper
- dash cayenne pepper

Directions
1. Mix all ingredients in a sealable plastic container or Ziploc freezer bag. Let sit for at least 4 hours. Then toss the steak

on the barbeque or campfire grill. Delicious! Wrap some potatoes in foil and cook in the fire as well.

Balsamic Vinegar Chicken

Ingredients
- 4 boneless, skinless chicken breast halves
- 3/4 c balsamic vinegar

Directions
1. lace the chicken and balsamic vinegar in a zip-top bag. Squeeze out as much of the air as possible when sealing. Place in refrigerator and marinate 4-12 hours (longer is better). Remove chicken from marinade and discard remaining liquid. The dark color of the vinegar will make the chicken appear almost brownish-gray. Don't worry - it'll be fine. Place chicken on grill over medium heat or you can pan fry covered over medium heat adding water to cover bottom of pan. Cook until no longer pink in center and juices run clear.
2. This goes well with rice, pasta or bread and a salad. Leftovers are great chunked into a big fresh salad with a light vinegarette dressing.

Bar B Que Mushrooms

Ingredients
- button mushrooms, washed and cleaned
- 1 16 oz. package of bacon
- barbecue sauce

Directions
1. Cut slices of bacon in half. Cut mushrooms in quarters or halves . Wrap bacon around mushrooms and either insert a wooden toothpick or place on a skewer. Place on grill. Coat with barbecue sauce when about done.

Barbecue Sandwiches

Makes: **7**

Ingredients
- 1-1/2 c chopped celery
- 1/2 c chopped onion
- 1/2 c ketchup
- 1/2 c barbecue sauce
- 1/2 c water
- 1 Tbsp vinegar
- 1 Tbsp worcestershire sauce
- 1 Tbsp brown sugar
- 1/2 tsp chili powder
- 1/2 tsp salt
- 1/4 tsp pepper
- 1/4 tsp garlic powder
- 2 pound(s) cooked and shredded beef brisket
- 6 -8 sandwich buns

Directions
1. Combine all ingredients except the beef and bring the sauce to a boil. Simmer sauce for 5 minutes, and then add shredded beef. Simmer at least 20 minutes longer after adding the beef and spoon over split sandwich buns of your choice.

Barbecued Chipped Ham Sandwich

Ingredients
- 1 c Heinz ketchup
- 1 c Classic Coke
- 1 pound(s) chipped or thinly sliced ham

- 4 - 6 sandwich buns

Directions
1. Combine first three ingredients in pot and stir over low heat until heated through. Serve on sandwich buns. Makes 4 to 6 sandwiches, depending on how high you pile it. Serve with a side of chips and fresh fruit.

Barbecued Chopped Ham Sandwich

Ingredients
- 1 c Heinz ketchup
- 1 c Coke - use only Classic Coke
- 1 pound(s) thinly sliced or chopped ham
- 4- 6 sandwich buns

Directions
1. Combine first three ingredients and stir over low heat until heated through. Serve on sandwich buns. Makes 4 to 6 sandwiches, depending on how high you pile it.

Bar-B-Que Bean Bake

Ingredients
- 1 pound(s) ground beef
- 1 pound(s) bacon
- 1 large onion, chopped
- 4 Tbsp mustard
- 4 Tbsp molasses or 1/2 cup brown sugar
- 3/4 tsp pepper
- 2 16 oz. cans red kidney beans, with juice
- 2 16 oz. cans pork & beans, with juice
- 2 16 oz. cans butter beans, drained
- 1/2 c ketchup
- 1/2 c bar-b-que sauce
- 1 tsp salt
- 1 tsp chili powder

Directions

1. Cook bacon, drain and chop. Cook beef and onion. Drain off fat. Mix all of the above ingredients together well. Simmer for 30 minutes stirring occasionally or put in Dutch oven and place on hot coals for 45 minutes, stirring occasionally. (At home, bake 1 hour at 350 degrees). Cut recipe in half for smaller family dish.

BBQ Bacon-Wrapped Stuffed Shrimp

Ingredients
- 30 10-ct Gulf shrimp - BIGGER is better!
- 1 jar horseradish, course
- 1 c Monterey Jack cheese
- 1/2 c Asiago cheese
- 1 jar BBQ sauce
- 2 pound(s) bacon

Directions
1. Peel and de-vein shrimp. Soak round toothpicks in water. Split shrimp down the outside, being careful not to cut all the way through. Combine cheeses in small bowl. Stuff split with horseradish, then cheese. Wrap shrimp with bacon and secure with toothpick. Grill and baste with BBQ sauce until bacon is done. Do not overcook. DELICIOUS!
2. Tip: If smaller shrimp are used, half bacon length-wise and pre-cook slightly to prevent the shrimp from becoming over-cooked.

BBQ Baked Beans

Ingredients
- 1/4 pound(s) bacon
- 1 medium onion
- 4 cloves garlic

- 4 cans navy beans
- 1 c strong black coffee
- 1/4 c dark brown sugar
- 1 Tbsp molasses
- 1 1/2 Tbsp Gulden's brown mustard
- 1/2 c BBQ sauce
- 1 tsp Tabasco sauce
- salt and ground black pepper

Directions
1. Heat 12" Dutch oven over medium heat for 2 minutes, add bacon and cook until lightly browned. Stir in onion, cook until softened. Add garlic and stir. Add beans, coffee, brown sugar, molasses, mustard, BBQ sauce, and Tabasco. Bring to a low boil, then cover with lid and simmer about 1 hour over low heat on high hook. Kitchen directions: Bake at 400° for 20 minutes, reduce heat to 350° for additional 35 minutes.

BBQ Beef Sandwiches

Ingredients
- 3 -5 pound(s) beef chuck roast
- 12 oz. jar chili sauce
- large jar of dill pickles

Directions
1. Brown the roast on both sides. Place in crockpot or dutch oven. Pour chili sauce and dill pickles (including juice) over the roast. Cook 6-8 hrs on low heat or until meat falls apart. When done shred meat with a fork. Mash the pickles into the meat and combine well. Serve on buns.

BBQ Country Style Ribs

Ingredients
- country style ribs, usually 2 - 3 per person
- beer of your choice - preferably strong

- barbecue sauce - we like Bulls Eye Sweet Hickory Smoke

Directions
1. Place ribs in large stock pot, pour beer over until completely covered. Cook on medium high heat (or over campfire) until boiling, then lower heat and cover. Cook for 2-3 hours, depending on pot size and number of ribs. The longer they cook, the more tender they will be, but you don't want them TOO tender to move around on grill.
2. Drain ribs, then place on grill rack or in large baking dish. For baking, baste with bbq sauce, then place covered pan in oven and bake at 350 for 30 minutes to 1 hour. For grilling, place on grill, baste with bbq sauce.. Grill each side approximately 7-10 minutes - adjust according to grill temperature. Serve with plenty of napkins!

Bbq Pitas

Makes: **4**

Ingredients
- 3/4 pound(s) thinly sliced beef or pork from the deli, cut in 1/2 inch strips
- 2/3 c barbecue sauce
- 4 thin slices smoked cheddar, Swiss, or Monterey Jack cheese with jalapeno peppers from the deli, cut in half
- 4 large pita bread rounds, split crosswise to form pockets
- alfalfa sprouts, tomato slices and/or sliced dill pickles

Directions
1. In a medium saucepan combine meat and barbecue sauce. Cook, covered, over medium heat till heated through, stirring occasionally.
2. Place a cheese slice half inside each pita bread half. Spoon about 1/4 cup of the meat mixture into each pita bread half.

Have each camper add the toppers they choose for a personalized pita dinner.

BBQ Potato Chips

Ingredients
- potatoes, cut into slices
- olive oil
- Mrs. Dash seasoning

Directions
1. Slice potatoes 1/4" thick. Lay them on a plate, brush one side with olive oil. Season to taste. I like Mrs. Dash and throw them on the hot grill, oiled side down. Brush the other side with oil, and season. Turn them after about 3 minutes and grill another 3 - 4 minutes.

BBQ Ribs

Makes: 4

Ingredients
- 1/2 c brown sugar
- 1/2 c apple butter
- 1/4 c bourbon
- 1/4 c cider vinegar
- 1/4 c apple cider
- 2 Tbsp Dijon mustard

Directions
1. Always remove membrane from the back of the ribs. Mix rub ingredients together and rub all over both sides of ribs. Let rub do its magic for 4 hours or more in the refrigerator. Put onion, ginger, cinnamon & apple cider in large roasting pan and mix until evenly distributed place ribs in roasting pan.

Cover with foil and cook over medium heat for 2 hours. While ribs are cooking in roasting pan, mix BBQ sauce, grill ribs over indirect medium heat for an additional hour brushing BBQ sauce on lightly every 15 minutes. Use smoking chips at this point if you like (sweeter chips are better).When ribs are done, cover with plastic wrap for ½ hour before serving. While ribs are cooling in a covered pan, take remaining BBQ sauce and a ½ cup of the roasting sauce and bring to a boil and let simmer until fairly thick. When done, serve on the side. Use a charcoal grill with a lid or over a fire. These are simply the best sweet ribs you ever tasted.

Bean & Cornbread Casserole

Ingredients
- 1 onion (chopped)
- 1 green pepper (chopped)
- 2 garlic cloves, minced
- 1 can red kidney beans
- 1 can pinto beans
- 1 can diced tomatoes
- 1 can tomato sauce
- 1 tsp chili powder
- 1 tsp black pepper
- 1 Tbsp prepared mustard
- 1 tsp hot sauce
- 1 c self-rising cornmeal
- 1 1/4 c milk
- 1 can cream-style corn
- 1 large egg
- 3 Tbsp vegetable oil
- 3 Tbsp butter

Directions

1. Pour oil into 14" Dutch oven and heat; sauté onion, bell pepper and garlic until tender. Add undrained kidney beans and pinto beans. Add diced tomatoes and juice, tomato sauce and seasonings. Cover and cook for 30 minutes. In mixing bowl, combine cornmeal, corn, milk, egg and butter. Spoon evenly over cooked bean mixture. Cover and cook over medium heat on medium hook for 35 minutes. Add top coals and continue to bake for approx. 25 minutes until cornbread is done. Kitchen directions: bake about 1 hour at 350°

Beef in the Wild

Ingredients
- 2 pound(s) ground beef
- 4 6 oz. cans Dawn Fresh Mushroom Steak Sauce
- 2 7 oz. cans pieces and stems mushrooms (drained)
- toasted bread

Directions
1. Cook ground beef over fire in skillet until no longer pink. Add the mushrooms and gravy and combine. Serve over toast. Easy, hearty, inexpensive, and delicious. Kids love it.

Beefy 5 Can Soup

Ingredients
- 1 pound(s) ground beef
- 1 small onion, finely chopped
- 2 cans Campbell's Minestrone soup
- 1 can corn
- 1 can Ranch Style beans
- 1 can Ro-Tel

Directions

1. Brown the ground beef in a pot. Drain on paper towels. Cook onion in drippings or oil added to the pan. Add the beef back to the pot. Pour in cans of soup, corn, beans and Ro-tel. Cook until hot and bubbly. Taste before adding any additional seasoning. Great with biscuits or cornbread!

Big Jim's Camping Beans

Ingredients
- 1 pound(s) bulk breakfast sausage (crumbled and cooked)
- 1 pound(s) ground beef (crumbled and cooked)
- 1 large onion
- 1 bell pepper
- 2 jalepeno peppers
- 1 can butter beans
- 1 can kidney beans
- 1 can green beans
- 1/2 c K.C. Masterpiece BBQ sauce
- 3 Tbsp dark brown sugar

Directions
1. Dice and sauté onion, bell pepper and jalepeno pepper with meat. In either a crock pot or baking dish, add beans, BBQ sauce and brown sugar. Cook in crock pot on high until thoroughly heated thru or in an oven at 375 degrees for 45 minutes. Serve and enjoy as side dish or main dish.

Black Bean Soup

Ingredients
- 2 cans black beans, drained and rinced
- 1 can beef broth
- 1/2 jar salsa
- 2 tsp cumin

Directions
1. Mix together and heat. Top with sour cream, diced green onion, and saltines.

Blair's Campfire Stew

Makes: 23

Ingredients
- 1 pound(s) sirloin
- 4 red potatoes
- 1 red onion
- 1-2 c vegetables
- 1 tsp salt
- 1 tsp ground black pepper
- 3 Tbsp butter

Directions
1. Preheat your grill to medium heat. Measure out 2 or 3 sheets of aluminum foil in 2-foot lengths, and layer one on top of the other (or a large aluminum grilling bag is easier). Layer the meat (cut in small chunks), sliced potatoes and onion and vegetables in the center, sprinkle with salt and pepper, and dot with butter. Wrap into a flattened square and seal the edges. Place aluminum wrapped package over medium heat and cover. Cook for approximately 40 minutes, turning once. Serve hot right off the grill.

Bob's Simple Skillet Supper

Ingredients
- 1/2 pound(s) link sausage
- 1 green pepper, seeded and sliced into strips
- 1 large onion, sliced
- 3 - 4 red potatoes, cut into chunks
- salt and pepper

Directions
1. Preheat skillet while slicing the onion and pepper. Slice sausages in half lengthwise so they will lie flat in the pan and cook more quickly and evenly. Spray pan lightly with cooking spray. Place sausage in hot pan and brown on all sides. Add onion and pepper -cook until they begin to soften. Place potatoes on top of vegetables. Season as desired with salt and pepper. Cover, reduce heat and simmer until potatoes are soft and no pink is left in sausage. stirring occasionally. If you want a crisp crust on the potatoes, remove lid and raise heat during the last 10 minutes of cooking.

Bourbon Steak (Or Chicken) Marinade

Ingredients
- 4-5 Ribeye steaks (or any beef) or Chicken (Boneless, skinless)
- 1/2 c Worcestershire Sauce
- 3 Tbsp Soy Sauce
- 1/2 tsp grated fresh ginger
- 1/2 c bourbon
- 1/4 c vegetable oil
- 3 cloves of garlic (pressed or minced)
- 1 medium onion (quartered)
- 4 Tbsp brown sugar

Directions
1. Before leaving to camp: mix all of the marinade ingredients together. Put meat and marinade in a ziplock freezer bag, and put in the RV refrigerator. Let marinate while traveling to your destination (at LEAST a good 3 hours is best). While your spouse is setting up camp, you can throw the meat on the grill (or campfire rack). Cook until juices run clear, or to desired doneness.

Bratwurts & Swiss

Ingredients
- Italian sausage or Johnson's Bratwursts and cheese
- your favorite cheese slices

Directions
1. Place Italian Sausage/Johnson's Bratwursts on a stick and cook over the fire (be sure to turn often) until thoroughly cooked. Place in hot dog bun and cover with a slice of your favorite cheese (I prefer Swiss cheese) YUM YUM - Eat on the go or on your plate with a few chips for a fast meal.

Broccoli Cole Slaw

Makes: **12**

Ingredients
- 16 oz prepared broccoli mix
- 1 bunch(es) green onions
- 1 package Ramen Noodles
- 1/2 c cashews
- 1/2 c sunflower seeds
- 1/2 c sugar
- 1/3 c vinegar
- 1/4 c oil

Directions
1. Mix slaw mix, onions, and broken dry noodles, then add the nuts. Mix the Ramen Noodle seasoning packet with the remaining ingredients for the dressing. Toss and serve. (May be made ahead of time).

Broccoli-Chicken Casserole

Ingredients
- 2 10 ounce package of broccoli cuts

- 2 cans boned chicken
- 2 cans undiluted cream of mushroom soup
- 1/4 c mayonnaise
- 1 tsp lemon juice
- 1 c shredded cheese

Directions
1. Boil and drain broccoli (not too done). Arrange in dish and top with chicken. Pour sauce of soup, mayonnaise and lemon juice. Top with shredded cheese. Bake at 350 degrees for 35 minutes.

Brownie's Chili, Cheese & Rice

Ingredients
- 1 large jar Bush's Chili (with beans or without)
- 1 - 2 packages Uncle Ben's Ready Rice
- 2 packages finely shredded Mexican cheese

Directions
1. Mix chili with cooked rice. Top with cheese. Bake at 350 deg. until cheese is melted and lightly browned. OR mix all ingredients together and heat until hot and cheese is melted. Serve with tortilla chips or soft tortillos.
2. Extra Toppings: top with chopped fresh onions, sliced black olives, crumbled tortillo chips.

Brunswick Stew

Ingredients
- 3 large smoked ham hocks (sliced 1" thick)
- 3 pound(s) stewing chicken (cut up)
- 2 pound(s) beef stew meat
- 2 bay leaves
- 1 tsp thyme, parsley
- 3 stalks celery
- 2 onions (cut in wedges)

- 1 Tbsp black peppercorns
- 2 Tbsp Durkee Six-Pepper Blend
- 2 cans tomatoes (cut up)
- 2 c carrots (peeled and chopped)
- 2 c celery (chopped)
- 2 c onions (chopped)
- large potatoes (diced)
- 2 c lima beans (frozen)
- 3 c corn (fresh off the cob)

Directions
1. Add ham hocks, chicken and beef stew meat to 14" deep or 16" Dutch oven. Add bay leaves, thyme, parsley, celery stalks, onion wedges, Six-Pepper Blend and peppercorns. Simmer covered until chicken and beef are thoroughly tender, about 2 hours. Remove meat and set aside to cool. Strain the stock and discard veggies and herbs. Skim off some of the fat. Add tomatoes, carrots, chopped celery, onions, potatoes, lima beans and corn to strained stock. Simmer uncovered until all vegetables are tender, about 30 to 45 minutes. Bone chicken and remove pieces of ham hock from the bone. Return meat to pot. Add more water if needed to make more soup. Simmer for 10 to 15 minutes and season with salt and pepper. Serve with cornbread and enjoy!

Bunless Hot Dogs

Ingredients
- 1 Can Wolf Brand Chili with Beans, Heated
- Grilled Franks, 2 per person, sliced in bite size pieces
- Mustard, Catsup or/And Mayo if desired
- Sweet India Relish or dill if preferred
- Grated Cheddar Cheese
- Fritos

Directions

1. Grill Franks and slice. Heat chili. Put about 2 franks in a bowl, Add Chili, Dribble with mustard, Mayo or catsup as desired. Add some relish. Sprinkle with cheese and with Fritos and eat. Betcha can't eat just one.
2. Serve with Salad if desired. Easy and quick. Less Carbs.

Burger & Veggie Pouches

Ingredients
- 4 hamburger patties
- 1 onion (sliced)
- 1 can mushroom soup
- potatoes
- squash
- butter
- seasoning to taste

Directions
1. Place hamburger patties on foil. Cover with a layer of onions and mushroom soup. Fold foil into pouch. On a second piece of foil, slice potatoes 1/2 inch thick and alternate layers with onions topping with a few slices of butter and your choice of seasoning. Slice squash and add to potatoes. Wrap up foil. Throw it all on the Webber or camp fire. Wait one hour turning every 15 minutes.

Burn-side taters

Ingredients
- 4 baking potatoes, sliced thin
- 1 c mild cheddar cheese
- 1 sweet onion
- 1 c shredded carrots
- salt and pepper

Directions

1. Layer ingredients equally on 6 greased (spray on vegetale oil) squares of aluminum foil. Fold foil in a butcher wrap to seal. Place on hot grill about 30 minutes or until potatoes are throughly cooked. (potatoes will be slightly burned on the bottom) Hence the name! Enjoy!

Cabbage Lasagna

Ingredients
- 1 1/2 pound(s) lean ground chuck
- 1 pound(s) sausage or 1 tube sausage
- 1 medium cabbage
- salt and pepper to taste
- 1 can tomato soup
- 1 can cream of mushroom soup
- 2 8 ounce packages of shredded cheese

Directions
1. Cook and drain meat . Cut up cabbage, then cook and drain. Add soups to meat in a 9X12 pan. Preheat oven to 400 degrees. Layer cabbage, meat mixture, and cheese, repeat, then cook until cheese is melted (about 15 minutes).

Cabbage Salad

Makes: 7

Ingredients
- 1/2 large head of cabbage, shredded
- 4 green onions, sliced
- 1/2 green pepper, finely chopped
- 1/2 c slivered almonds, toasted
- 1/2 c sunflower seeds
- package of Chicken flavored Ramen noodles, uncooked

Directions

1. Combine the shredded cabbage, onions, green pepper, almonds and sunflower seeds in a large bowl. Break the ramen noodles up into smaller pieces and set aside. Save the flavor packet for the salad dressing.

Cajun Shrimp Gumbo

Ingredients
- 1 onion
- 1 green pepper
- 2 cloves garlic
- 1/4 c butter
- 1 corn (32 ounces frozen or 1 can)
- 1 can Rotel Diced Tomatoes & Green Chilies
- 1 Tbsp sugar
- 1 tsp salt
- 1/4 tsp pepper
- dash cayenne pepper
- 1/2 large can canned milk (make sure to use canned milk)
- 1/4 c chopped green onions
- 2 pound(s) shrimp (shelled or canned or frozen)
- corn starch

Directions
1. Chop the onion, green pepper and garlic cloves. Sauté onion, pepper & garlic in butter to a tender crisp. Add corn, tomatoes, sugar, and salt & pepper and heat for 10 minutes. Add canned milk and green onions and heat 4-5 minutes. Add shrimp at the right time, (adjust the time if using raw or cooked shrimp), you do not want to over cook the shrimp. Make a paste using the cornstarch and some water to thicken. Serve over Rice. If you don't like spicy, use Rotel mild diced tomatoes & green chilies and cut back on the Cayenne. This recipe is very versatile because you can use canned corn, canned shrimp and you can prepare the veggies at home.

California Egg Crunch

Ingredients
- Egg
- Bacon (cooked crispy and crumbled)
- Cheese Nips (crumbled)

Directions
1. Scramble the eggs and cook them, add bacon and cheese nips right before the eggs set, continue to cook until eggs are done. Sit back and enjoy. The amount of eggs and bacon and cheese nips all depends on how many you are feeding.

Camp Beef Brisket

Makes: **10**

Ingredients
- 1/4 c paprika
- 2 Tbsp garlic, minced
- 1 Tbsp thyme
- 1 Tbsp basil
- 1 Tbsp oregano
- 1 Tbsp dried parsley
- 1 Tbsp ground black pepper
- 1/2 tsp cayenne
- 1/2 tsp ground nutmeg
- 2 Tbsp Tabasco sauce
- 2 Tbsp Worcestershire sauce
- 3-4 pound(s) beef brisket

Directions
1. Mix all the spices together, then dry rub the meat. Coat with Tabasco and Worcestershire sauce, rubbing in carefully not to displace spices. Refrigerate for 3 to 5 days - if time

permits. Place meat trivet in bottom of Dutch oven large enough to hold brisket. Place brisket (fat side up) on trivet. Cover and hang low over the fire to get the pot hot. When the meat starts to sizzle, raise to the highest hook and cook over low fire for approximately 12 hours. Go for a ride, take a nap, do some fishing and cook the brisket overnight. Low and slow is the key to a good, juicy brisket that is fork tender, and that's just all there is to it! When it's done, throw it on the grill to crispy the outside, slice and pour the juices from the pot over the meat.

Camp Bread

Ingredients
- 1 16 oz. package hot roll mix
- 1 Tbsp snipped fresh rosemary or basil or 1 Tsp. dried rosemary or basil, crushed
- 1/2 c shredded Parmesan cheese
- cornmeal

Directions
1. Prepare hot roll mix in a 10-inch Dutch oven according to package directions, adding the rosemary or basil and 1/4 cup of the Parmesan cheese to the dry ingredients (omit kneading step). Remove dough.
2. Grease the Dutch oven and sprinkle with cornmeal. Place dough in Dutch oven. Using greased hands, gently press dough evenly into the bottom of Dutch oven. If desired, use a small knife to make a decorative pattern on top of the bread. Sprinkle with remaining 1/4 cup Parmesan cheese. Cover and let rise in a warm place until dough nearly doubles (30 to 40 minutes).
3. Cover Dutch oven and arrange 8 to 10 hot coals around the edge of the Dutch oven and 10 to 12 hot coals on the lid. Bake for 20 to 25 minutes or until golden, rotating the Dutch

oven a half-turn halfway through cooking. Makes 12 servings.

Camp Fire Rainbow Trout

Ingredients
- Rainbow trout
- squeeze butter or margarine
- lemon slices
- salt and pepper

Directions
1. Prepare your freshly caught pan size Rainbow trout with squeeze margarine, or butter, slices of lemon, salt and pepper. Wrap in foil (enough to wrap around several times) Place in camp fire or on the grill (close to the coals) for about 7 minutes on each side. Test fish for flakiness and cook more if needed. Enjoy!

Camp Stew

Ingredients
- 2 pound(s) hamburger
- 1 can stewed tomatos
- 1 can corn
- 1 c elbow macaroni
- 1/2 c chopped onions
- 1 c water
- 1/4 pound(s) cheddar cheese

Directions
1. Brown hamburger in dutch oven, kettle, or skillet. Drain. Stir in tomatoes, corn, macaroni, and water. Cook until hot. Just before serving add cheese.

Camp Stove Goulash

Ingredients
- 1 pound(s) ground meat (turkey, beef or chicken)
- 1 sweet onion
- 1 green or red pepper
- 1 16 ounce can diced tomatoes (Mexican flavor)
- 1 16 ounce can garbanzo beans
- 1 can corn
- ketchup (optional)
- rice

Directions
1. Brown the beef, onions and pepper in large skillet or pan. Chop up the onion and green or red pepper. Add the tomatoes, garbanzo beans (drained), corn and a squirt of ketchup (if desired) and serve over rice (Our favorite is the boil in the bag kind).

Camo Tacos

Ingredients
- 1 jalapeno pepper
- 1 medium onion
- 1 can Rotel
- 1 package taco seasoning
- 1 can black beans or 1 bag instant black beans
- 2 packages Chicken of the Sea white chunk chicken
- tortillas
- salsa

Directions
1. Drain Rotel and mix with diced veggies, chicken and beans in pot. Warm over stove or fire and add taco seasoning. Cook 15 minutes or until veggies are soft. Warm tortillas on lid of pot or over fire in foil. Put chicken mix in tortillas and add salsa.

Camp Taters

Ingredients
- 4 potatoes
- 1 red bell pepper
- 1 green bell pepper
- 1 onion
- salt and pepper
- 1/4 stick of butter

Directions
1. Slice poatoes in 1/4 inch horizontal slices. Slice 1/2 of red and 1/2 of green peppers lengthwise in thin strips, slice 1/2 onion in small strips. Melt butter and mix all ingredients in large bowl. Season to taste, wrap in double foil and grill until brown on both sides.

Camper Casserole

Ingredients
- 2 c water
- 1 package Butter & Herb Noodles with sauce
- 1 6 oz. can chunk ham
- 1 14 oz. can peas or 10 oz. bag frozen peas
- 1 tsp dried minced onion

Directions
1. Bring water to a boil in 2 qt saucepan. Add the rest of the ingredients. Continue to cook over medium heat for about 8 to 10 minutes or until noodles are cooked. Be sure to stir occasionally to keep from sticking to pan.

Camper Goulash

Ingredients
- 1 pound(s) lean ground beef
- 1 can cream of mushroom soup
- 1 can tomato soup
- 1 box elbow macaroni (16 oz)

Directions
1. Brown ground beef until fully cooked. Add both soups and stir it all together. Prepare macaroni per package directions. Drain. Stir into beef and soup mixture. Cover and let stand for 5 minutes. Stir again and serve.

Camper's Beans

Ingredients
- 1 Large can of butter beans-drained
- 1 Large can baked beans
- 1 Large can kidney beans-drained
- 1 Large can Pork n Beans-drained
- 8 Strips of bacon cut-up
- 1 Medium Onion
- 2 c Shredded Cheddar Cheese
- 1/3 c Brown sugar or pancake syrup
- 1/3 c Ketchup
- 2 Tbsp Worcestershire Sauce

Directions
1. Brown bacon on stove top with 1 medium onion. Mix all ingredients together and put in crock pot on low for 6 to 8 hours.

Camper's Luau Chicken

Makes: **2**

Ingredients

- 3 envelopes onion cup-a-soup
- 1 8 oz. can crushed pineapple, undrained
- 1 whole chicken breast, split
- 1 small green bell pepper, cut into strips
- 2 18-inch square pieces heavy-duty aluminum foil

Directions
1. In a small bowl, combine onion cup-a-soup and pineapple.
2. For each serving, place half the chicken, onion-pineapple mixture and green pepper on foil. Wrap loosely, sealing edges airtight with double fold. Place on grill, seam-side up, over hot coals or high heat, and cook 45 minutes, or until chicken is tender.

Camper's Pizza Skillet Delight

Ingredients
- 1 pound(s) ground beef
- 1 can (4 oz.) sliced mushrooms
- water
- 1 can (8 oz.) pizza sauce
- 3 c Uncle Ben's Quick Brand Rice
- 1 large green pepper, chopped
- 1 1/2 tsp salt
- 1 tsp oregano
- 1/4 c grated Parmesan cheese
- 6 thin slices Mozzarella cheese

Directions
1. Brown meat in a 10-inch skillet; drain. Drain mushrooms, reserving juice. Add water to juice to make 2 cups liquid. Add liquid, pizza sauce, rice, mushrooms, green pepper, salt and oregano to beef; stir. Bring to boil. Reduce heat, cover and simmer until liquid is absorbed, about 5 minutes. Sprinkle Parmesan and arrange Mozzarella on top of beef-rice mixture. Cover skillet and heat for 2-3 minutes, or until cheese softens.

Campers Stew

Ingredients
- hamburger patty
- onion (sliced)
- white potatoes (sliced)
- sweet potatoes (sliced)
- baby carrots
- 1 Tbsp butter
- salt & pepper to taste

Directions
1. Place in foil pouch. Put on Grill or in Oven or even over a campfire for about 40-45 minutes or until burger is done and vegetables are tender.

Campfire Chicken and Vegetables

Ingredients
- 2 boneless, skinless chicken breasts
- 1 bag baby carrots
- onions
- potatoes
- 1 cream of chicken soup

Directions
1. You will need heavy duty aluminum foil. Get your coals really hot and fire red. While they are heating, prepare your chicken. Tear off foil big enough to hold chicken and large vegetables. Place chicken breasts on foil and add 1/2 the can of soup. Cube the potatoes and onions. Place cut up potatoes, onion and your carrots on top of the chicken. Fold foil tightly, be sure to seal so the soup doesn't leak out. Place on fire grate or directly on hot coals. Cook for approximately 30 minutes, turning at least once.

Campfire Chicken and Veggies

Ingredients
- boneless skinless chicken breast
- red potatoes
- baby carrots
- green peppers
- onion
- corn
- italian dressing (or spice mixture of your choice)

Directions
1. You will need Reynolds foil grill bags. Cut everything up, put it in a bag, and cover it with italian dressing (usually about half a bottle per foil bag), roll the bag down, throw the grate over the campfire or directly on hot coals. Cook until potatoes are tender and chicken is cooked. ENJOY!!!

Campfire Chicken Pot Pie

Ingredients
- 4-6 Whole Boneless Chicken Breast (or chicken of choice)
- 1 Cream of Chicken, Mushroom or Broccoli Soup
- 1/2 c water or milk
- 1 Can Mushrooms
- 2 Bags of Califlower, Broccoli and Carrots (frozen vegetable mix)
- 1 large onion
- Olive Oil
- Butter
- Salt & Pepper (or seasoning of choice)
- Cooking Spray

Directions

1. Spray the bottom of a medium sized foil baking pan with the cooking spray. Line the bottom of the pan with sliced onions. Spread the sliced mushrooms and frozen vegetable mix over the onion layer. Mix soup and water (or milk). Spread soup mixture over vegetables. Add a little olive oil and butter. Season chicken and place on top of mixture. Using heavy duty aluminum foil, cover the pan completely from side to side and end to end wrapping all the way over the bottom of the pan to create a good seal. Put on camping rack over hot coals. Check for doneness after approximately 1 hour (cooking time will vary depending on the heat from the coals). You may place directly on the coals, but the mixture may stick to the bottom of the pan. Serve with your choice of bread.

Campfire Chicken

Ingredients
- 3 chicken breasts, cubed
- 4 medium potatoes, cubed
- 1 16 oz. package baby cut carrots
- 1 medium sweet onion, cubed
- 1 can cream of mushroom soup
- 1/2 stick butter

Directions
1. Make 2 or 3 small bowls with foil wrap. Put chicken, potatoes, carrots & onion in bowls. Mix soup with 1 can water. Add to bowls. Add 2 pats butter per bowl. Cook over open fire or on grill for 15-20 minutes or til potatoes are tender.
2. This easy meal is made easier if you cube all ingredients and store in separate containers before going camping! This

recipe can also be made in RVs. Bake in dish in oven at 400 degrees for 30 minutes.

Campfire Chili with Hamburger

Makes: **5**

Ingredients
- 1-1/2 pound(s) hamburger
- 1 onion, chopped
- 1 clove minced garlic
- 1 14.5 oz. can stewed tomatos
- 1 16 oz. can pinto beans
- 1 8 oz. can tomato sauce
- 1 c ketchup
- 2 c water
- 4 tsp chili powder
- 1 tsp cumin
- 1 Tbsp sugar
- 1/2 green pepper, chopped
- 1/2 jalapeno, diced without seeds
- salt and pepper to taste

Directions
1. Cook hamburger, onions and garlic together over medium high heat until hamburger is cooked thoroughly. Then add remaining ingredients in the order listed above and mix. Simmer chili over medium low heat for 15 to 20 minutes and serve.

Campfire Chili

Ingredients
- 1 can hot chili red beans
- 1 can chili seasoned chopped tomatoes
- 1 can tomato sauce

- 1 small can tomato paste
- 1 can tomato juice
- 2 pound(s) hamburger
- 1 onion
- 1 small carrot
- 1 small potato
- chili powder
- tabasco sauce

Directions
1. Shred the carrot and the potato. Add chili powder and Tabasco sauce to taste. Brown hamburger, then add the rest of the ingredients. Cook over fire embers for at least 4 to 6 hours with a light boil. Serve and Enjoy!

Campfire Corn on the Cob

Ingredients
- corn on the cob (do not husk)
- water
- 1/2 - 1 c sugar (optional)
- butter
- salt (optional)

Directions
1. Mix water and sugar in a clean bucket, cooler or large pan (add enough water to cover corn). Add the corn to the water mixture and soak for one-two hours. Remove corn from water and place on campfire or grill, turn often to avoid over burning of the husk, cook for approximately 20-30 minutes or until tender, remove corn from fire. Peel back husk and silk, spread with butter and/or salt. Now your ready to eat the sweet, delicious, steaming hot corn.

Campfire Corn

Ingredients
- corn on the cob
- 2 Tbsp butter
- salt and pepper

Directions
1. Rub butter on each corn cob and salt & pepper, then wrap each individual cob in aluminum foil. Place on BBQ grill.

Campfire Dinner

Ingredients
- 1 pound(s) lean hamburger
- 6 potatoes
- 3-4 carrots
- 1 medium to large onion
- 4 slice(s) bacon
- seasoning

Directions
1. Make hamburger into 4 patties. Slice the potatoes, carrots, and onion. Place 1 hamburger pattie, 1/4 of the potatoes, carrots, and onions on a piece of aluminum foil, large enough to wrap around all ingredients. Add 1slice of bacon, halved. Season with your preferred seasonings. Wrap all ingredients in the foil, and seal well. I then wrap it again. Place in a bed of coals for approximately 15 minutes, turn and cook for another 15 minutes. Cooking time varies, so just keep checking. Variations can include mushrooms, peas, or anything else desired.

Campfire French Fries

Ingredients
- 1 medium potato, cut into strips

- seasoning salt and pepper to taste
- 1 Tbsp Parmesan cheese
- 1 Tbsp margarine
- 1 Tbsp bacon bits

Directions
1. Place potato on large square of heavy duty foil. Sprinkle with seasoning salt, pepper and cheese; toss to coat. Dot with margarine; sprinkle with bacon bits. Seal foil, leaving steam vent on top. Grill over hot coals for 30-45 min or until potatoes are tender, turning occasionally.

Campfire Onion

Ingredients
- 1 large onion
- 1/4 c butter
- 1 beef bouillon cube
- 1 Tbsp Worchester sauce
- 1 tsp fresh garlic

Directions
1. Hollow out the center of the large onion, add butter, bouillon, worchester and garlic. Cover completely with aluminum foil and place over the campfire on a rack for approximately 45 minutes.

Campfire Pizza's

Ingredients
- 1 jar pizza quick sauce
- 1 8 oz. package of mozzarella cheese
- 1 roll Italian sausage, cooked and crumbled
- 1 small package pepperoni, cut into small pieces
- 1/2 bell pepper, chopped
- 1/2 onion, chopped

- 1 stick butter
- 1 loaf bread

Directions
1. Warm pie iron in the fire for couple of minutes. Open only one end of the butter and run all over inside the pie iron. next place a slice of bread on each open side. Mix all other ingredients and add about 2 Tbsp. of meat mixture fold back together then cook in fire until toasted on each side. It takes about 5 minutes to cook. Repeat process over and over !!

Campfire Potatoes and Onions

Ingredients
- 2-3 pound(s) white or red potatoes
- 1 medium to large onion
- 6-8 slice(s) bacon
- 1-2 Tbsp olive oil

Directions
1. Cut onion and potatoes into chunks. Lay out foil into a "pan". Lay 3 to 4 slices of bacon on the bottom, then add onions and potatoes. Add oil and top with remaining bacon. Wrap tightly. Grill 20 to 25 minutes and then flip foil packet over and cook an additional 2- minutes.

Campfire Potatoes

Ingredients
- potatoes
- butter
- salt

Directions

1. Wash potatoes and add butter and salt, then wrap in aluminum foil and place on grill

Campfire Roasted Turkey

Ingredients
- 1 8-12 pound Turkey
- salt and pepper
- seasonings

Directions
1. Season the turkey with salt and pepper and a seasoning blend (if desired). Place a meat rack in the bottom of a 14" deep Dutch oven, spray with oil. If stuffing turkey, pack loosely. Place turkey on the rack. The sides of the turkey should not be touching the Dutch oven. Cover and start on low hook over medium fire. When the turkey begins to cook (steam and sizzle), raise to higher #2 hook and continue cooking. When meat thermometer reaches nearly done stage, remove from fire, add top coals to brown and finish cooking. Roasting time for 8 to 12 lb. turkey is 2-3/4 to 3 hours, if stuffed 3 to 3-1/2 hours. Turkey is done when internal temperature reaches 180°F, stuffing 165°F.

Campfire Squash

Ingredients
- butternut squash
- baby carrots
- butter
- brown sugar

Directions
1. Take a butternut squash- not too small- cut the top off like a little pumpkin---scoop out a little well not too much as you are also going to eat the squash---put in a package of baby carrots, butter, cut up about 1/3 of a stick and brown sugar

to the top---put the little top on, wrap in tinfoil---put right on the roaring campfire and about an hour later you have 2 delicous vegetables--scoop out carrots and then mash the squash or just eat out of it as if it were a bowl.

Campfire Stew with Hamburger

Ingredients
- 1 pound(s) ground beef
- 1/2 large onion
- 1 large can of Campbell's Vegetable Soup

Directions
1. Brown ground beef and onion. Drain. Add vegetable soup and heat till hot. This can be made in a dutch oven over a fire, on the camper stove or in an electric skillet.

Campfire Stew

Ingredients
- 1 pound(s) ground beef
- 1 small onion, chopped
- 1 small can stewed tomatoes (optional)
- 1 can (10 3/4 oz.) Campbell's chicken gumbo soup
- 1 can Veg All
- salt and pepper to taste
- garlic powder to taste (optional)

Directions
1. Brown ground beef and onion, Drain Grease. Add rest of ingredients, stir and cover for 10 to 15 minutes. Serve with buttered bread.

Campfire Stir Fry

Ingredients
- 1 package Hilshire Farm Lite Polska Kielbasa
- 4 beef tenderloin fillets
- 1 red pepper
- 1/2 small onion
- 1/4 c olive oil
- 1/2 c butter
- salt and pepper to taste

Directions
1. Slice the Polska Kielbasa and meat into bite size pieces. Slice the pepper and onion. Put into a disposable aluminum 13x9 inch pan and cook over the fire until meat is cooked to your liking!
   Great served with potatoes and mushrooms:

- 1/2 stick butter
- 1tbs olive oil
- 1 15oz can sliced white pototoes
- 1 8oz or 4oz can sliced mushrooms
2. Cook over fire in round or square aluminum cake pan. Cook only until heated through.

Campfire Sweet Potatoes

Ingredients
- 1 large can of sweet potato's drained
- 1/2 c apple butter
- 1 Tbsp honey
- 1 Tbsp brown sugar
- 1 tsp lemon juice
- half a stick of butter
- 1/2 tsp cinnamon or nutmeg

Directions

1. Cut a big piece of foil to make a packet. Drain sweet potatoes and mix apple butter, honey, brown sugar , lemon juice. Pour over potatoes, cut up butter and dot potatoes. Sprinkel cinnamon or nutmeg over potatoes. Wrap in foil, grill in oven or on grill for 10 minutes, carefully remove and ENJOY!!!!!

Campfire Tacos

Ingredients
- 4 medium potatos
- 2 pound(s) precooked ground beef
- 1 package shredded cheese
- 1 package taco seasoning
- 1 can black olives
- 1 package sour cream

Directions
1. Cube potatoes and put in a foil packet put in fire for 1/2 hour.
2. While cooking potatoes, place thawed meat in a pan on camp stove and add 1 cup water and taco seasoning. When potatoes and meat are done. Place potatoes in a bowl and add meat, top with cheese and all other taco items.

Campfire Vegetable Packet

Ingredients
- 2 potatoes, peeled and cubed
- 1 yellow squash, cubed
- 1 zucchini, cubed
- 1 Tbsp margarine or butter
- 1 tsp tarragon (or your favorite herb)
- salt and pepper to taste
- 1/2 c White Zinfandel wine

- 1/2 c shredded Swiss cheese

Directions
1. Combine vegetables and pour onto aluminum foil. Sprinkle with spices and cheese. Pour wine over all. Cook over fire or grill for 20 minutes.

Campfire Zucchini

Ingredients
- 1 zucchini per person, approximately
- 2 eggs, beaten (egg beaters can be used)
- 1/2 c seasoned bread crumbs
- 3 Tbsp olive oil
- salt and pepper to taste

Directions
1. Cut zucchini diagonally into small slices. Dip slices into beaten egg then dip slices into seasoned bread crumbs until completely covered. Season with salt and pepper. Place zucchini slices on heavy duty aluminum foil. Drizzle slices with olive oil. Grill approximately 2-3 minutes each side.

Campground Chicken Salad

Ingredients
- 1 5 oz. can Swanson Boned chicken or turkey, cut up
- 2 hard-cooked eggs, chopped
- 1/4 c chopped sweet pickle
- 2 Tbsp minced onion
- 1 tsp mustard
- salt
- pepper

Directions
1. Lightly mix chicken, eggs, pickle, onion and mustard; season to taste with salt and pepper. Serve as a sandwich filling or on crackers.

Campgruond Goodies

Ingredients
- Hot Dogs
- Sweet Baby Rays barbeque sauce

Directions
1. Cook hot dogs on a grill and just before they are done coat them several times with SWEET BABY RAYS barbecue sauce. Gives them a wonderful flavor and helps keep them moist.

Campground Stew

Ingredients
- 1 pound(s) ground beef (or any meat you like)
- 1 carrot (or any vegetable of your choice, chopped)
- 1 can whole peeled potatoes (cut in half)
- 1 green pepper, chopped
- 1 onion, chopped
- salt and pepper
- barbecue or hot sauce (optional)

Directions
1. Fold a large piece of aluminum foil in half. Pile on ground beef, add potatoes and your choice of vegetables, add onion. Salt, pepper & sauce to taste. Roll up sides of foil so they are tight. Place along sides of fire pit and cook on one side until sizzling, turn over and cook on other side. Even kids can do this! What a fun dinner!

Camping Burritos

Ingredients

- 2 pound(s) ground beef
- 1 can pork and beans
- 1 can pinto beans with jalapenos
- 1 small onion
- 1 package grated cheddar cheese
- 1 bottle hot sauce
- 1 package large flour tortillas

Directions
1. Combine Ground Beef and 1 Small Onion (diced) in skillet, brown, remove grease. Add 1 Can Pork and Beans, and 1 Can Pinto Beans w/ Jalapeno. Cook through, stirring frequently. Warm Flour Tortillas, turning often, so as not to burn. Fill Flour Tortillas with Meat and Bean mixture, cheese and hot sauce. Wrap Tortilla like an envelope, fold in half, fold both sides in, then fold top.

Camping Potatoes

Ingredients
- 4 large potatoes
- 2 celery stalks
- 4 cubes butter
- 1 medium onion
- parsley
- salt and pepper
- water

Directions
1. Cut aluminum foil into 4, 12X12 inch squares. Dice potatoes, onions and celery into 1 inch cubes or smaller. (1" for potatoes, smaller for celery and onions). Put all diced items into a bowl, add add salt, pepper, and parsley to your liking. Mix up until all ingredients are thouroughly combined. Place equal amounts from the bowl onto seperate pieces of the

aluminum foil squares you cut. Add butter to your liking to each group. Wrap up foil around your mixture leaving a small opening. Pour about a 1/4 cup of water into each and crimp the hole shut. Place on grill or over the fire for about 20 minutes or until potatoes are soft. Empty into a bowl and enjoy.

Camping Spaghetti

Ingredients
- 1 pound(s) hamburger
- onion
- salt and pepper
- 2 large cans of Franco American spaghetti

Directions
1. Brown hamburger, flavoring with some onion, salt & pepper, etc. Drain, add a couple lg. cans of Franco American spaghetti. Serve with a salad or bread and butter. Cooking it like this totally changes the flavor of the canned spaghetti. I like to think of it as a camper's hamburger helper. We love it! It can be cooked on the grill or stove.

Camping Stew

Ingredients
- 1 package hot dogs, sliced or 1 pound browned hamburger
- sauteed onions (optional)
- 1 can Bean and Bacon soup
- 1 can corn
- 1 can lima beans
- 1 can potatoes (diced small)
- 1 can green beans

- other canned vegetables of choice

Directions
1. Bring this to a boil over campfire or other heat source and simmer. Season to taste. Stew is even better when made a day ahead and let the flavors meld. Enjoy!

Camp-Out Chicken

Ingredients
- 4 boneless, skinless chicken breasts
- 1 large green bell pepper
- 1 medium white onion
- 1 bottle Italian dressing

Directions
1. Cut chicken, pepper and onion into bite-sized pieces. Place in zip lock bag and pour bottle of Italian dressing over contents. Allow to marinate overnight in cooler. Place on cast iron griddle on grate over open fire and cook for 30 minutes or until chicken is no longer pink inside. Can use pork or beef instead or in addition to chicken for variety.

Camp-Out Tomatoes

Ingredients
- 4-5 large tomatoes
- 1 medium sized red onion
- 1 bottle red-raspberry viniagrette dressing

Directions
1. Cut tomatoes and onion into bite-sized pieces. Place in zip-lock bag and pour in entire bottle of dressing. Allow to marinate overnight in cooler. Pour contents of bag into pot on camping stove or over fire and allow to boil/simmer for 30 minutes.

Can-Do Potato Bean Salad

Ingredients
- 1 16 oz. can of sliced potatoes, drained and rinsed
- 1 1/4 c garbanzo beans, drained and rinsed
- 1/2 c sliced celery
- 1/4 c sliced pitted ripe olives
- 2 Tbsp sliced green onion
- 1/4 c Italian salad dressing
- 1/2 c cherry tomatoes, quartered
- 1 yellow or green sweet pepper, halved and seeded, or lettuce leaves

Directions
1. In a large bowl, combine potatoes, garbanzo beans, celery, olives and onion. Add salad dressing and toss gently to coat. Cover and chill at least 2 hours. At serving time, stir in the cherry tomatoes, spoon salad mixture into sweet pepper halves or serve on lettuce leaves.

Carrot and Egg Salad

Ingredients
- 1/2 head of iceberg lettuce chopped
- 2 carrots, shredded
- 3 hard boiled eggs, chopped

Directions
1. Toss lettuce, carrots and eggs together in large bowl. Then mix up the following dressing in a separate bowl:
2. 1-1/2 teaspoon grated onion
3. 1/2 cup miracle whip or mayonnaise
4. 1/3 cup Catalina dressing
5. Pour dressing over salad mixture and toss. Serve immediately.

Cashew Apple Salad

Ingredients
- 1/2 c powdered sugar
- 1/4 c mayonnaise
- 2 medium apples, chopped
- 1 can (10 oz.) salted cashews

Directions
1. In a bowl, combine powdered sugar and mayonnaise until smooth. Stir in apples and cashews. Serve immediately.

Cheddar spam and potatoes

Ingredients
- 1 can Spam, diced
- 4 medium potatoes, diced
- 1 small onion, diced
- 1 8 oz. package shredded cheddar cheese
- 1/2 stick margarine

Directions
1. Place in hot bag or foil diced spam, potatoes and onion and margarine. Place on grill of hot coals or very small fire. Let cook until potatoes are done, approximately 1/2 hour to 45 minutes turning over occasionally not to burn. When done, open bag or foil and sprinkle with shredded cheese.

Cheddar Tator Tot Casserole

Ingredients
- 1 pound(s) ground beef
- 1 can Campbell's Cream of Mushroom soup
- 1 can Campbell's Cheddar Cheese soup
- 1 bag frozen tator tots

Directions

1. Brown the ground beef in a skillet and drain the grease. Stir in the cream of mushroom and cheddar cheese soup with the beef until it is well blended. Pour mixture into a 9 x 13 pan and top with frozen tator tots. Bake for 50 minutes in a 350 degree oven.

Cheese on the Cob

Ingredients
- 1/2 c mayonnaise
- 5 ears of corn, husked and cleaned
- 1 c fresh shredded Parmesan cheese
- chili powder
- salt
- black pepper

Directions
1. Prepare grill. Brush a thin layer of mayonnaise on corn. Sprinkle the corn with cheese, light amount of chili powder, salt and pepper. Wrap each ear of corn in foil, and place each on the grill. Turn occasionally and cook for 10 minutes or until kernels begin to brown. Serve warm......Enjoy.

Cheesy Sausage Skillet

Ingredients
- 1 pound(s) cooked polish or kielbasa, cut into 1/2 inch pieces
- 1/2 c chopped onion
- 1 package Cheesy Scalloped Potatoes
- 1/8 tsp ground red pepper
- 2 1/3 c water
- 2/3 c milk
- 1 Tbsp butter or margarine
- 2 c frozen or canned mixed vegetables

Directions

1. In skillet or electric frying pan, cook sausage and onion until sausage is browned and onion is tender, stirring frequently. Drain. Add potato slices, contents of sauce packet from potatoes. ground red pepper, water, milk and butter, mix well. Bring to a boil. Reduce heat; cover and simmer 10 minutes, stirring occasionally. Stir in vegatables; simmer an additional 7 to 10 minutes or until potatoes and vegetables are tender, stirring occasionally.

Cheesy Veggie Chowder

Makes: **8**

Ingredients
- 4 c chicken broth
- 8 stalks celery (sliced)
- 4 carrots (sliced)
- 2 medium potatoes (peeled and cubed)
- large onion (chopped)
- 1 tsp black pepper
- 2 c whote kernel corn (frozen)
- 1/4 c butter
- 3/4 c all-purpose flour
- 2 c milk
- 2 c cheddar cheese (shredded)

Directions
1. Add vegetables to chicken broth and bring to a low boil for about 20 minutes. While vegetables are cooking, melt butter in a skillet. Slowly add flour, stirring constantly. Add milk and stir until thoroughly mixed. Stir in cheese until completely melted. Add cheese sauce to vegetables. Stir. Cook at a medium low heat until vegetables are of desired tenderness.

Cherry Fruit Salad

Ingredients

- 1 can cherry pie mix
- almond extract
- 1 can fruit cocktail
- 1 c whipped cream
- nuts (optional)

Directions
1. Pour pie mix into bowl. Pour 1 capful almond extract over this. Let it stand for a while. Drain fruit cocktail and add to pie mix. Add the whipped cream (sweetened as usual) and nuts to mixture. Keep chilled until ready to serve.

Chicken & Rice

Ingredients
- 1 1/2 pound(s) chicken, cut into cubes
- 1 bottle light Italian dressing
- 1 small box minute rice

Directions
1. Cook the cubed chicken in a frying pan with half the bottle of italian dressing. Drain excess when chicken is fully cooked. Pour desired amount of rice in pan with the chicken, add second half of dressing and add enough water to cover the rice. Bring water/rice mixture to a quick boil and shut off heat & cover, let sit for a few minutes and serve.

Chicken Almondine

Ingredients
- 1 c cooked chicken
- 1 c chopped celery
- 1/2 c Minute Rice
- 1 can Cream of Mushroom Soup
- 1/2 c real mayonnaise
- 1/4 c diced onion
- 1/4 c butter

- 1/2 c slivered almonds
- 1 c crushed cornflakes or Special K cereal

Directions
1. Mix the chicken, celery, rice and onion. Blend the soup and mayonnaise together. Add to chicken mixture. Place in casserole dish. Mix butter (melted and cooled), slivered almonds and crushed cornflakes or Special K and spread on top of chicken mixture. Bake at 350 degrees for 40 minutes.

Chicken & Corn Soup

Ingredients
- 1 can, corn
- 1 can, creamed corn
- 1 l chicken stock
- 3 chicken fillet (finely diced)
- 3 eggs

Directions
1. Bring chicken stock to boil, add corn and chicken and boil for twenty minutes. Beat eggs and then drizzle into soup stirring constantly. Simmer for five minutes and serve.

Chicken and Stuffing

Ingredients
- 6-8 chicken breasts or thighs
- 1 can Cream of Mushroom soup
- 2 c sour cream
- 1/2 pound(s) mushrooms
- 1 can or package chicken broth
- 1 Tbsp butter
- 1 8 ounce box Stove Top Stuffing with seasoning

Directions

1. Brown chicken and cut into bite-size pieces. Layer in bottom of 11 x 13 casserole. Mix sour cream and cream of mushroom soup together. Spread over top of chicken. Sauté mushrooms in butter and layer over sour cream mixture. Add broth to stuffing. Mix well and spread over the top. Bake at 350 ° for 1 hour uncovered.

Chicken Asparagus

Ingredients
- 4 chicken breasts
- 1 can Cream of Mushroom Soup
- 1 can Aspargus Spears
- 2 tsp salt
- 1/2 tsp pepper
- 1/2-1 tsp garlic salt
- 4 slice(s) provolone cheese

Directions
1. Tear off four squares of aluminum foil approximately 6 inches long. Wash chicken and remove skin if desired. Spray each sheet of foil with Pam oil. Place chicken breast in center of sprayed foil (bone side down) and sprinkle salt, pepper, and garlic salt on. Place one slice of cheese on top of spices, (one slice per breast), and then add the asparagus. Wrap sides and ends together and bake in the oven at 300 degrees for approximately 90 minutes or on the grill until the chicken is done. This is very low in carbohydrates.

Chicken Broccoli Casserole

Ingredients
- 1/4 c butter
- 1/4 c + 1 Tablespoon of flour
- 1 cream of chicken soup
- 1 c milk or chicken broth
- 1 c shredded cheese

- 2 Tbsp mayonnaise
- 1 tsp mustard
- 2 c cooked chicken (2 chicken breasts)
- 3 c cooked broccoli (1 head and stalk cut up fine)

Directions
1. Melt butter. Add flour, chicken broth or milk, mayonnaise, and mustard. Cook on low until thick. Pour in pan. Add cut-up chicken. Sprinkle with cheese and press down into sauce. Bake at 325 degrees for 35 minutes.
2. Hint: I cook cut up onion and garlic powder in my chicken. Then remove chicken and cooked broccoli in the same broth. I add extra broth to make it more creamy.

Chicken Cacciatore

Ingredients
- 1 frying chicken
- 1 bell pepper
- 1 white onion
- 8 oz sliced mushrooms
- 3 cloves of garlic
- 1/4 c olive oil
- 1 large jar of spaghetti sauce
- 1 Tbsp dry oregano
- 1/4 c fresh basil
- 1/2 c red wine
- salt and pepper

Directions
1. Cut up chicken into pieces, chop bell pepper, onion, garlic, and fresh basil. Heat olive oil in Dutch Oven or over coals until hot. Brown onions and garlic, add chicken pieces (turning to brown on both sides) and red wine. Stir in bell pepper, mushrooms, spaghetti sauce and salt & pepper and herbs. Cover with lid and add coals to the top. Cook 30 to 45 minutes. Serve with/over white rice or pasta. I like to prep all my ingredients into plastic bags at home. You can also add zucchini, eggplant, fresh tomatoes, squash, Italian sausage or anything you like.

Chicken in A Bag

Ingredients
- 1 pound(s) chicken breast
- 2 c rice

- 1/2 pound(s) frozen peas
- 1/2 pound(s) shredded cheddar cheese

Directions
1. You will need one small roll of aluminum foil (heavy gauge is better) and 4 sticks (about 1/2-1 inch in diameter). At home, cut chicken breast into cubes and fully cook in a skillet. Season with lemon pepper if you like. Cook rice, remove from pot and let cool. In a large container, combine chicken, rice, frozen peas, and shredded cheddar cheese. Cover and refrigerate. At dinner time, scoop each serving onto the middle of a 2 ft. long piece of aluminum foil. (four servings = four pieces of aluminum foil). Wrap the mixture into the foil by folding the foil longwise (so that it stays about 2 ft. long). Wrap the tail ends of the aluminum around a heavy stick and warm each wrapped mixture over a campfire until the cheese melts. The foil cools rapidly and can be unwrapped easily from around the sticks and from around the mixture. You could also add cashews, canned mushrooms, and/or soy sauce depending on the tastes of the group.

Chicken kabob wraps on flat bread

Ingredients
- 1/4 c olive oil
- 2 Tbsp lemon juice
- 1 tsp oregano
- 1/2 tsp thyme
- pepper
- hot sauce to taste
- 2 chicken breasts cut into kabob chunks
- 1 pkg ceasar salad mix

Directions

1. Kababs: Mix together first 6 ingredients. Marinade the chicken in the sauce for at least 2 hours. While the chicken is marinading, make the bread. Put the chicken onto skewers and grill for 4-8 minutes or until cooked through. Oil a griddle and heat. When the griddle is hot, cook each flatbread, one side at a time until lightly browned. Add more oil if the bread begins to stick

Chicken Mole

Ingredients
- Flour
- Vegetable Oil
- Cumin
- Salt (optional)
- Oregano
- California Chile powder or New Mexico Chile powder (which is hotter)
- Chicken Broth
- Chicken Breasts

Directions
1. Boil the chicken breasts and set aside, let the broth stand so the fat will sink to the bottom. In a frying pan, add about 2 tablespoons of vegetable oil. Heat and then remove from heat, add some flour to make a paste, then add your choice of Chile powder, enough to make it paste still, but not lumpy. Return to mid heat, gradually stir in the chicken broth, slowly with a whisk, getting out the lumps. Thickness will come while it cooks. Add a touch of salt, cumin and oregano to taste. About ½ teaspoon to start. Use two forks to shred the chicken to your choice or cut into cubes. Then add the chicken to the mole and let it simmer for about 10 minutes. Enjoy with flour tortillas for breakfast, lunch or dinner!!

Chicken or Pork Chops Deluxe

Ingredients
- 4 skinless, boneless chicken breasts or 6 center cut pork chops
- 1 c rice
- 1 c water
- 1 can Cream of Mushroom soup
- 1/2 c skim milk
- 4 oz. sliced mushrooms
- 1 package frozen broccoli, thawed and drained

Directions
1. Mix rice, water, milk, mushrooms and broccoli in a baking dish that will fit into your convection oven. Place meat on top and then spread the soup over entire dish. Bake at 350 degrees for 30 minutes. Serve with a salad and enjoy.

Chicken Pie

Ingredients
- 2 Pillsbury pie crusts
- 2 chicken breasts, boiled
- 1 can peas and carrots or mixed vegetables (drained)
- 1 can cream of chicken soup
- 1/4 c milk

Directions
1. Bake at 400 degrees for 30 to 35 minutes or until crust is browned. Makes 1 9" pie.

Chicken Pockets

Ingredients
- 1 tube ready made crossiants

- 1/2 c finely chopped onion or green onion
- 1 c cheese (reserve 1/2 cup for sauce)
- cooked chicken
- cream of chicken soup
- milk

Directions
1. In a bowl shred the chicken into pieces, add the cheese and onion and mix together. Open the tin of crossiants and add a bit of the chicken mixture to each one and roll it up. Place on the cookie sheet and cook per the package instuctions. In a sauce pan open and add a can of cream of chicken soup and one can of milk and add about 1/2 cup cheese for a nice little cheesy sauce to cover the chicken pockets with.

Chicken Pot Pie

Ingredients
- 1 large can chicken meat
- 1 1/2 cans cream of chicken, mushroom or celery soup
- 1 large can of mixed vegetables with potatoes
- 1/2 can of milk
- 1 c shredded cheddar cheese
- 2 frozen pie crusts

Directions
1. Mix first five ingredients together and pour into one of the pie shells. Place other pie shell on top of mixture, press edges of pie shells together, and flute top shell. Bake at 350 degrees for 40 minutes.

Chicken Salad for Two

Ingredients
- 1 can chicken, drained
- 1 8 oz. can crushed pineapple in juice
- 1 7 oz. can mushrooms, drained
- 3 Tbsp mayonnaise

Directions
1. In a bowl combine Chicken, Pineapple with juice & Mushrooms. Add Mayonnaise and mix well.

Chicken Salad

Ingredients
- chicken breast or canned chicken, shredded
- mayonnaise
- ranch dressing
- crushed pecan pieces
- salt and pepper to taste

Directions
1. Mix well using 1 part ranch dressing to 2 parts mayonnaise to make salad moist. Serve on crackers or use as sandwich spread. For people watching their carbs this recipe is great for cheese or lettuce roll ups.

Chicken Salsa Stir-fry

Ingredients
- 1 pound(s) skinless chicken breast tenders
- 2 Tbsp olive oil
- 1 c thick and chunky mild salsa
- 1 frozen stir fry vegetables (12-16 oz. package)
- 1/2 tsp garlic powder (optional)
- 1/2 c mozarella cheese

Directions

1. Mix vegetables, olive oil, and salsa in a bowl. Place in a piece of heavy duty foil (18 inches in length), sprayed with non-stick cooking spray. Place chicken tenders, singly, on top of vegetable mix and sprinkle with garlic powder. Seal foil to form a long rectangular shape. Place over an open fire and cook approximately 20-30 minutes depending on how hot your fire is. Check every 10 minutes or so. When chicken juices run clear, sprinkle cheese over the chicken and loosely seal foil until cheese is melted. Feeds 4. You could also serve this with rice.

Chicken Sandwiches

Ingredients
- 1 can chicken
- 1 can cream of mushroom soup (10 oz)

Directions
1. Open cans and pour into a pan or put in a microwave safe bowl. Heat through. Put on buns. These make quick sandwiches and serve with potato chips or veggies and dips. This is very delicious. Also, if you have a big crew, you can buy the family size cream of mushroom soup and a big can of chicken.

Chicken Sausage Bake

Ingredients
- 1 package Chicken Sausage fully cooked

- 1 large green, yellow and red pepper, drained
- 1 large sweet onion
- 4-5 baking potatoes, peeled

Directions

1. Cut everything up into large bite size pieces. Mix with pepper and garlic salt to taste. Drizzle w/ olive oil (any oil will work). If using campfire to cook make sure there are about 3-4 layers of foil and a little extra oil so everything won't burn or stick. If using oven in RV you can actually spray everything in a baking dish with Pam. Cook until everything is tender.

Chicken Vegetable Medley

Ingredients

- 2 1/2 - 3 lb frying chicken, cut up
- 2 Tbsp flour
- 1/4 c Wesson oil
- salt and pepper
- 1 can Hunt's Manwich Sauce
- 1 c sliced celery
- 1 c diced carrot
- 1 tsp salt
- 1 clove garlic, minced
- 1/3 c white wine or water

Directions

1. Coat chicken with flour seasoned with salt and pepper. Brown well in Wesson oil. Remove excess fat. Combine remaining ingredients and pour over chicken. Cover skillet and simmer 45 minutes.

Chicken Wing Dip

Ingredients
- 2 c or 4-6 breasts of cooked chicken
- 8 oz cream cheese (softened)
- 8 oz ranch dressing
- 8 oz hot sauce
- 1 package of cheddar cheese (shredded)
- 1-2 bags of tortilla scoop chips or large nacho chips

Directions
1. Cook chicken in microwave or oven until done. Let cool. Shred into very small pieces using two forks or your hands. Spray a 9x13 pan or deep dish pie plate with cooking spray. Mix cream cheese with ranch dressing and hot sauce until smooth or most of the lumps are gone. Add in shredded chicken, mix well. Pour into pan and sprinkle with cheddar cheese. Bake @ 350 for 30 minutes or microwave for 8-10 minutes. Use tortilla chips for dipping.

Chicken with Wine and Capers

Ingredients
- 6 boneless skinless chicken breasts
- flour
- salt and pepper
- olive oil
- 1/2 c chopped onion
- 2 garlic cloves, chopped
- 1/4 c chicken broth (you may use 1/2 cup if you don't wish to use wine)
- 1/4 c dry white wine (don't use cooking wine)
- 2 Tbsp Dijon mustard
- 3 tsp drained capers
- 1 Tbsp corn starch mixed with 2 T. water

Directions
1. Prepare your starch before you get started. Preheat saute pan on medium high heat. Pour enough olive oil into pan to coat bottom. Coat one side of chicken with flour and place into pan. Salt and pepper other side of each breast as it browns. Cook chicken until golden-about five minutes on each side. More or less depending on the thickness of the chicken. After chicken is cooked thoroughly, remove from pan to a plate and cover with foil. Reduce heat to medium and to the pan, add the onion and garlic. You may have to add a little more olive oil. Saute until the onion is translucent and then add the wine and chicken broth. Allow to boil and reduce by 1/2. To this mixture, whisk in the mustard, capers and while the sauce is boiling, add the cornstarch. Pour sauce over the chicken and serve. You may also wish to add mushrooms while sauteing the onions, or add one can of artichokes when you add the capers.

Chicken/Veggie Pouches

Ingredients
- Chicken (boneless/skinless)
- Veggies
- Seasoning
- Foil

Directions
1. Take boneless, skinless chicken breast or strips and add whatever veggies you wish to whatever seasonings you wish and wrap in individual sheets of aluminum foil. Add to grill and cook approx 45 minutes. Enjoy! Each person will have their own wrapped goodness.

Chili Bean Bake

Ingredients
- 1 can baked beans
- 1 can chili
- 1/4 c brown sugar
- 8 hot dogs sliced thin
- 1/2 tsp salt
- 1/4 tsp pepper

Directions
1. Mix all ingredients together and place in oven proof casserole. Bake for 35 minutes at 350 degrees. Serve as a meal with corn bread or canned brown bread or serve as a side dish.

Chili Bean Soup

Ingredients
- 2 c dried pinto beans
- 1 pound(s) ground beef
- 1/2 large onion, chopped
- 2 cloves garlic, minced
- 7 oz. diced green chilies
- 1 tsp salt
- black pepper to taste

Directions
1. In crock pot, cover beans with water, add salt and cook on low overnight. In the morning, crumble and brown ground beef. Add meat, onion, garlic and chilies to beans. Taste and adjust salt and pepper to your taste. Raise crock pot to high and let simmer for 3 hours. For a little extra kick, add a pinch or two of cayenne pepper.

2. For campfire cooking, cook beans in dutch oven until done. Add remaining ingredients and simmer, covered, for another 2 hours.

Chili cheese dog casserole

Ingredients
- 1 can of chili
- 1 package hot dogs (sliced)
- 1 package frozen tatar tots or french fries
- 8 oz shredded sharp cheese or 1 package of any cheese
- 1 Tbsp mustard
- 2 Tbsp chopped onion

Directions
1. Preheat oven to 375 degrees. Place the tatar tots in a 9x11 baking pan, spread out evenly. Add the sliced hot dogs, squeeze the mustard over, then sprinkle the onions on top. Next, spoon the chili on top, spreading as much as possible. Top with the shredded cheese, and bake for 20 minutes in a preheated oven, depending on your oven. Serve with fresh fruit, and enjoy!

Chili Cheeseburger

Ingredients
- 1/2 pound(s) Ground Aged Angus Beef
- 1 tsp Minced Garlic
- 1/2 c Chopped Onion
- Salt
- Pepper
- 2 Large Jalepenos (one sliced thin, the other whole)
- 1/4 c Shredded Lettuce
- 1 slice(s) Large Tomato

- 1/4 c Shredded Monterrey Jack
- 1/4 c Shredded Mild Cheddar
- 1 c Wolf Brand Chili
- 1 Large Toasted Hamburger Bun

Directions
1. Mix Ground Sirloin, minced garlic, half of the onion, salt and pepper to taste. Divide the meat in half and pat out into two ¼ lb patties. Cook to your taste. Place lower half of bun on plate, tomato and lettuce, last half of Chopped Onion, sliced Jalapeno and pour Chili over this. On top of this place Monterrey Jack Cheese, meat patty, Cheddar Cheese, meat patty. Place upper half of bun on top and top it off with the other Jalapeno. You may use Mustard and Mayo to taste.

Chili Dog Casserole

Ingredients
- frito corn chips
- chili
- hot dogs
- shredded cheese

Directions
1. In individual bowls, start with frito corn chips on bottom of bowl. Add warmed chili, followed by hot dogs (cooked on the fire, of course) cut up, followed by shredded cheese, and topped with more frito corn chips. Super easy, and the kids LOVE IT!

Chili Dogs in a Blanket

Ingredients
- 10 6-inch flour tortillas
- 10 hot dogs
- 1 15 oz. can of chili with beans
- 1 1/2 c shredded American cheese

Directions
1. Place each tortilla on a sheet of heavy duty foil. Place hot dog in center of each tortilla. Top each with 2 TBS chili and 2 TBS cheese. Roll to enclose filling; secure with toothpicks. Wrap tightly with foil. Place on grill 4-6 inches from hot coals. Grill for 10 -15 min or until heated through. Serve with sour cream if desired.

Chinese Cabbage Slaw

Ingredients
- 1 head bok choy (shredded)
- 1 head Chinese cabbage (shredded)
- 8 green onions (diced)
- 1 carrot (shredded)
- 2 Tbsp butter
- 1/2 c sliced almonds
- 1/4 c sesame seeds
- 1/4 c vegetable oil
- 1/4 c sesame oil
- 6 Tbsp rice wine vinegar
- 1/2 c sugar
- salt and pepper (to taste)

Directions
1. Mix bok choy, Chinese cabbage, onions and carrots in a bowl. Melt butter in a skillet, add almonds and sesame seeds; sauté over medium high heat 5 minutes or until lightly

browned. Drain and cool slightly. Stir vegetable oil, sesame oil, rice wine vinegar and sugar into almonds and sesame seeds. Mix well until sugar is mostly dissolved. Toss with bok choy mixture and serve immediately.

Chinese chicken salad with chicken strips

Ingredients
- 1-2 packages pre-cooked chicken strips
- 5 - 6 oz. package sliced almonds
- 2 packages oriental flavor Top Raman noodles
- 1/2 c margarine
- green onions
- 1 head Napa cabbage
- 1/2 - 1 head iceberg lettuce
- 1 c cooking oil
- 1/2 c salad vinegar (or white wine)
- 1/2 c sugar

Directions
1. Cut chicken into bite size pieces. Crumble Raman noodles from both packages into 1/2 inch pieces. Melt margarine in large skillet. Add almonds and crumbled noodles and one package of Top Raman seasoning. Saute until golden brown. Set aside. Shred cabbage and lettuce into thin slices. Chop green onions.
2. For dressing, mix oil, vinegar, sugar and the other package of Top Raman seasoning (make dressing as early as possible, shake or stir so sugar can dissolve). Combine all ingredients in a very large bowl and toss to mix.

Chinese Chicken Salad

Makes: **2**

Ingredients
- 1 bag of prewashed salad
- 16 - 18 Tyson Popcorn Chicken nuggets, cooked and cooled
- 1 can mandarin oranges
- sliced almonds
- rice noodles
- T. Marzetti Honey Dijon Mustard salad dressing
- Bangkok Padang Peanut Sauce

Directions
1. Place the salad on 2 large plates or pasta bowls. Put the chicken and mandarin oranges on the salad. Add desired amounts of the dijon mustard and peanut sauce as dressings to the salad (careful--the peanut sauce is very spicy). Sprinkle with almonds and rice noodles. Serve with crusty bread.

Chinese Vermicelli

Ingredients
- 1 package vermicelli (cooked)
- 1/4 c sesame oil
- 1/4 c soy sauce
- 2 Tbsp hot chili sesame oil
- 2 Tbsp balsamic vinegar

Directions
1. Cook the vermicelli and in a mixing bowl, combine the rest of the ingredients together. Mix together with the noodles. Garnish with 1/2 cup toasted sesame seeds and 1 cup finely chopped green onions if desired.

Chuck Wagon Dinner

Ingredients
- 1 pound(s) ground beef
- 1 small onion, chopped
- 1-2 cloves garlic, chopped
- 4 - 6 small potatoes, chopped into small pieces
- 8 - 10 small mushrooms, chopped
- 1 can green beans
- salt and pepper
- worchestershire sauce

Directions
1. Form the meat into 4 burger sized patties (not too thick) and place each one on a large sheet of foil. Top each patty with some onion, garlic, potatoes, mushrooms and green beans. Sprinkle salt and pepper over each pile. Then drizzle a little worchestershire on each. Fold the packets so the seam remains on the top. (Fold tightly so the juices stay inside to cook everything.) Grill time depends on heat source, flip for last 5 minutes.

Chuck Wagon

Ingredients
- 1 pound(s) ground beef (extra lean)
- 1 can whole kernel corn
- 1 can diced tomatoes
- 1 c macaroni wagon wheels (or elbow macaroni)
- salt and pepper

Directions
1. Put macaroni in one quart of cold water and bring to a boil. Remove from heat. Brown ground beef, then drain any pools

of grease. Drain macaroni, then add the browned beef to it. Drain water from can of whole kernel corn and in with the macaroni and beef. Dump the whole can of tomatoes (with the liquid) into the mixture and bring to a boil. Remove from heat. Serve and season to taste.

Chunky Chili Chaser

Ingredients
- 1 can (19 oz.) Campbell's Chunky Beef Soup
- 2 tsp catsup
- 1 tsp mustard
- dash hot pepper sauce

Directions
1. In saucepan, combine all ingredients. Heat; stirring occasionally.

Citrus Rainbow Trout

Ingredients
- 1 slice(s) lemon
- 1 slice(s) orange
- mayonnaise
- 1 gutted rainbow trout
- dash lemon salt

Directions
1. Sprinkle lemon salt on the meat inside the body cavity. Place lemon and orange slices inside the fish. Cover the skin of the fish with mayonnaise and wrap in aluminium foil. Place directly on BBQ, set on med/high for forty minutes and turn once.

Civiche

Ingredients
- shrimp, approximately 60, cut into small pieces
- 2 c lemon juice
- 1/2 tsp garlic salt
- onion, chopped
- tomato, chopped
- cilantro
- 3 - 5 chili peppers, chopped
- 1/2 cucumber, chopped
- 1 avocado, pureed

Directions
1. Night before serving: soak shrimp, onion, garlic salt, & lemon juice in dish. Add other ingredients & mix. Serve with Tostito scoops.

Clam Chowder

Ingredients
- 4 oz salt pork (diced)
- 1 onion (finely chopped)
- 1/4 c diced celery
- 3 potatoes (diced)
- 1 c clam juice
- 1 c water
- 1/4 tsp ground thyme
- 2 c milk
- 2 c light cream
- 4 dozen large clams

Directions

1. Brown salt pork and remove from Dutch oven. In rendered fat, sauté onions and celery until tender. Add potatoes, clam juice, water, thyme, and salt and pepper to taste. Simmer uncovered until potatoes are tender. Stir in milk, cream, and clams. Heat through, but do not boil.

Corn Bread Salad

Ingredients
- cornbread mix
- 1 Tbsp sugar
- 1 bell pepper
- 1 medium onion
- 6 - 10 small tomatoes or two large tomatoes
- 1 jar of pickle cubes
- mayonnaise

Directions
1. Make one 12 inch skillet of cornbread, add 1 tablespoon of sugar to your recipe. Let this cool. Cut 1 bell pepper, 1 med onion, 6 to 10 small tomatoes or about 2 large ones into small pieces. Take one jar of pickle cubes and drain the juice. Mix juice with mayonnaise do not use salad dressing. Make this the consistancy of dressing. Crumble cornbread and start layering cornbread, pickles, onion, tomatoes and pepper. Put some

Corn Cassarole

Ingredients
- 4 cans shoe peg corn
- 1 stick butter
- 1 8 oz. package cream cheese
- jalapenos to taste (deseed, devein and chop fine)

Directions

1. Make one 12 inch skillet of cornbread, add 1 tablespoon of sugar to your recipe. Let this cool. Cut 1 bell pepper, 1 med onion, 6 to 10 small tomatoes or about 2 large ones into small pieces. Take one jar of pickle cubes and drain the juice. Mix juice with mayonnaise do not use salad dressing. Make this the consistancy of dressing. Crumble cornbread and start layering cornbread, pickles, onion, tomatoes and pepper. Put some of the dressing over each layer and add remaining dressing on top.

Corn Casserole

Ingredients
- 1 pound(s) can creamed corn
- 1 c Bisquick
- 1 beaten egg
- 2 Tbsp butter (melted)
- 4 oz chopped green chilies
- 2 Tbsp sugar
- 1/2 c milk
- chopped onions
- 1 pound(s) sliced Monterey Jack cheese

Directions
1. Combine corn, Bisquick, egg, butter, sugar and milk and mix together. Turn half of batter into greased 8 x 8" glass dish. Cover with chilies and cheese slices. Spread remainder of batter next. Bake at 400 degrees for about 20-30 minutes until golden brown.

Corn Chips

Ingredients
- 2 8-inch tortillas
- 2 Tbsp Olive oil
- coarse salt, regular or seasoned

Directions
1. Cut each tortilla into 8 wedges. Lightly brush each side with Olive oil. Put them in pan over fire or on stove. Flip when they begin to brown. When they are brown on both sides lightly sprinkle with salt.

Corn on the Cob with Bacon

Ingredients
- husked corn on the cob
- raw bacon slices
- parmesan cheese

Directions
1. Wrap a whole slice of bacon around each ear of corn after generously sprinkling on the parmesan cheese. Then wrap each cob securely in aluminum foil, twisting the ends. Cook on the rack over the campfire or on the grill, turning often, for about 35 minutes. No need for butter or salt due to the bacon.

Corn on the Cob

Ingredients
- 4 ears of corn
- butter or margarine
- salt and pepper

Directions

1. Remove husks from corn. Spread corn generously with butter or margarine and sprinkle with salt and pepper. Wrap each ear in foil, sealing and twisting foil around ends. Place on grill over hot coals for 15 to 20 minutes or till tender, turning often.

Corn Roasted In Foil on Coals

Ingredients
- corn on the cob
- butter or margarine

Directions
1. With husks: Remove outer husks on cob corn. Peel back the inner husks, but do not remove. Clean any silk and remove. Spread soft butter or margarine over the corn. Pull the husk back over the corn. Wrap in heavy -duty aluminum foil. Lay on the as gray coals for 20 to 30 minutes, turning once.
2. Without husks: Remove husks and silk. Place on piece of heavy-duty aluminum foil. Add 1 tablespoon of butter or margarine and 2 tablespoons of water. Wrap securely and lay on the coals or grill. Takes about 20 to 30 minutes to heat through.

Corn Roasted On Grill over Coals

Ingredients
- corn on the cob with husks
- butter or margarine
- salt and pepper to taste

Directions
1. Remove the large outer husks of cob corn. Turn back the inner husks, but do not completely remove. Clean any silk

and remove. Spread the corn with butter or margarine. Pull the husks back over the corn and tie with fine wire. Place over the hot coals or grill and turn frequently until heated through, about 20 to 30 minutes. Serve with salt and pepper and MORE BUTTER!

Corn Souffle

Ingredients
- 1 can whole kernel corn, drained
- 1 can cream corn
- 1 egg, lightly beaten
- 1 box Jiffy cornbread mix
- 1 c sour cream
- 1 cube butter

Directions
1. Lightly beat egg, add both cans of corn, sour cream, cornbread mix. Melt butter in glass pyrex square pan, pour mixture into butter, DO NOT MIX. Butter will come over the top of mixture. Bake 350 for 1 hour.

Crab Meat Appetizer

Ingredients
- 1 8 ounce white crab meat or 1/2 pound fresh (shelled)
- 1 15 ounce can grapefruit slices (in its own juice)
- 2 Tbsp ketchup
- 1 tsp horseradish
- 2 Tbsp mayonnaise
- 1 Tbsp white wine or water

Directions

1. Thoroughly drain crab meat and grapefruit, then mix together in a medium or large bowl and then transfer to serving dishes (4 to 6). Cover and refrigerate. Whisk or mix sauce ingredients with a fork, combining all ingredients well (increase or decrease horseradish to taste). Cover and refrigerate. Chill both ingredients in separate containers for 3-4 hours. Just before serving, pour approximately 1 and 1/4 Tablespoons of sauce on each individual serving and serve (diners should mix ingredients in individual dishes before eating).

Crunchy Oriental Coleslaw Salad

Ingredients
- 1/3 c light olive oil
- 1 package (3 ounces) chicken flavored Ramen Noodles
- 1/2 tsp garlic powder
- 1 package (16 ounces) shredded coleslaw mix
- 1 package (5 ounces) sliced almonds

Directions
1. Put coleslaw mix and almonds in a bowl, sprinkle garlic powder and seasoning packet from noodles over slaw mix. Heat oil in microwave for 1minute and pour over slaw and mix. Crush the noodles and mix in slaw. You can add sunflower seeds or any type of nuts that you like. This is a fast and easy side dish for burgers or hotdogs, or any type of sandwich when you are camping. You can mix everything but the noodles ahead of time add the noodles right before serving.

Cucumber Salad

Ingredients
- 3-4 large cucumbers, thinly sliced
- 4 large onions, thinly sliced
- 2 large green or red peppers, thinly sliced (optional)
- 1/4-1/3 c salt
- 2 c white vinegar
- 3 c sugar
- 1 Tbsp celery seed

Directions
1. Mix together the salt, vinegar, sugar and celery seed until the sugar is dissolved. Pour over vegetables; leave in bowl overnight. Put in jars and store in the refrigerator. Wait 3 or 4 days before eating. This will keep a LONG time.

Curry Chicken Salad

Ingredients
- 2 large cans of cooked white chicken breast (9.5 oz.)
- 1 large red delicious apple
- 1/2 c chopped pecans
- 1 Tbsp curry powder
- 1 c mayonnaise

Directions
1. Open and drain the 2 cans of chicken (fresh cooked chicken can also be used). Place the chicken in a bowl and flake with a fork. Cut the apple into bite size pieces in the same bowl as the chicken. Add the pecans and curry powder. Mix all this together with the mayonnaise. The amount of mayonnaise may vary depending on whether you like lots of mayonnaise in salad or not.
2. This may be served with fresh grapes, cantaloupe and crackers. A cantaloupe may be cleaned and quartered with the chicken salad served inside.

Dave's Sweet BBQ Corn on the Cob

Ingredients
- corn on the cob (do not remove or open husks)
- honey
- margarine or butter

Directions
1. Soak corn (with husks on) in a large pot of fresh water for about an hour. Pick off any loose husk pieces that may stick out into the fire. Place on campfire grate and cook, rotating periodically for about 40 minutes. Husks will be burnt looking. Remove husks & lather in margarine and honey! You'll never go back to boiling your corn again!
2. Tip: to avoid burns while removing the husks, dip your hands in cold water then quickly strip the husk.

Deluxe Steamed Green Beans

Ingredients
- fresh green beans
- 2 Tbsp butter
- 2 - 3 cloves garlic, minced
- 8 oz. fresh mushrooms, rinsed and quartered
- salt and pepper

Directions
1. Construct a dish out of heavy duty tin foil. Rinse and snap the ends off of one pound (more or less) of fresh green beans and heap on the tinfoil dish. Add fresh garlic, quartered mushrooms, butter (in chunks) and salt and pepper to taste. Seal up the whole dish tightly, using an extra piece of tin foil wrapped around the whole thing. (From experience, it is best to keep all seals facing up) Place on

your campfire grill over indirect heat, I.e. not over an open flame. Once you hear them steaming, allow to cook for 10 to 15 minutes. Open carefully, serve and enjoy! Can also add onion, zucchini, or squash if desired.

Dilled Peas & Potatoes

Ingredients
- 8 small new red potatoes (1-1/2 pounds)
- 1 pound(s) sugar snap peas (fresh or frozen)
- 1/2 c olive oil
- 6 Tbsp white wine vinegar
- 2 Tbsp fresh dill, minced
- 1/2 tsp salt
- 1/2 tsp freshly ground pepper
- 6 green onions (chopped)

Directions
1. Cook potatoes in Dutch oven in boiling water until tender; drain and thinly slice. Cook snap peas until crisp-tender; drain and plunge in cold water to stop cooking; drain again. Whisk together oil and next 4 ingredients. Add to sliced potatoes, snap peas, and onions, tossing gently to coat. Cover and chill 2 hours, or serve warm.

Doctored Up Pork & Beans

Ingredients
- 1 16 oz. can pork and beans
- 1/2 onion, chopped
- 2 tsp brown sugar, packed
- 1/4 tsp dry mustard

- 1/4 c ketchup
- 2 slices of bacon, chunked and fried until crispy

Directions
1. Combine all ingredients and simmer for 30 minutes. More bacon may be used if desired.

Dutch oven Stuffed Peppers

Ingredients
- 4 large green bell peppers
- 1 1/2 pound(s) hamburger
- 1 can Vegetable Beef soup
- 1 package Lipton Beefy Onion dry soup mix
- 1 egg

Directions
1. Cut the top off the green pepper and clean out. Retain the tops. Mix together all the ingredients, then form into 4 balls. Fill each green pepper with a hamburger ball and then replace the top of the pepper. Place the peppers on a wire rack in the bottom of the Dutch oven. Cover with the lid. Place 12 hot Briquettes under the Dutch oven, 10-12 an inch apart around the lid of the Dutch oven, and two on each side of the handle in the middle. Cook for 1 1/2-2 hours. Every 30 minutes add fresh hot coals to the bottom and top of the oven and rotate the oven one quarter of a turn. The tops of the peppers may turn dark brown, but cook until the meat reaches the doneness level you prefer.

Easy Barbecue Sauce

Ingredients
- 2 medium onions, sliced

- 3/4 c ketchup
- 3/4 c water
- 2 Tbsp Worcestershire sauce
- 2 Tbsp vinegar (white or apple cider)
- 1 tsp chili powder
- 1 tsp garlic powder
- salt and pepper to taste

Directions
1. Combine all in saucepan and simmer for 45 minutes.